The Religion of College Teachers

The Religion of College Teachers

THE BELIEFS, PRACTICES, AND RELIGIOUS PREPARATION OF FACULTY MEMBERS IN CHURCH-RELATED COLLEGES

By R. H. EDWIN ESPY

FOREWORD BY

CLARENCE P. SHEDD

ASSOCIATION PRESS, *New York*
1951

PRINTED IN THE UNITED STATES OF AMERICA

TO MY PARENTS
who have given
meaning to both
education and religion

FOREWORD

NEVER in this century has there been so much serious and creative discussion of the problems of religion in higher education as during the past decade. Books, conferences, faculty consultations, curricular changes, student discussions, chapels and chaplaincies, local faculty-student discussions—these are but a few evidences of the ferment of deep concern which cuts across all types of institutions and which breaks out in the most unsuspected places. In all this the church-related colleges have, or should have, a central place, because their history and charters have for two and a half centuries proclaimed the inescapable connection between religion and any higher learning worthy of the name.

Dr. Espy's study raises many disturbing questions regarding the implementation of the Christian purposes of these colleges. It does not attempt to provide all the answers to the central question of church college leadership but it gives some of the answers and poses basic issues for further study. It pictures a group of gifted teachers with real religious concern but it does not give indication of fresh thought and initiative on the part of the teachers that matches either their concern or the needs of our time. Our debt is very heavy to Dr. Espy for the facts and the issues that his study reveals.

Upon the church-related colleges rest grave responsibilities in these dark days. They are committed institutions and in a unique sense they have the opportunity to demonstrate for the rest of American higher education ways in which religion may be more integrally related to learning. With few exceptions they are small or moderate-sized institutions, hence they have the possibility of control of the totality of their life.

While we have deep gratitude for the present widespread interest and discussion, yet it is not out of place to suggest that higher education needs demonstration vastly more than it needs further discussion. A few colleges, possessing competent and illumined leadership, and seized by a big enough idea could, through experimentation, profoundly influence all of American higher education—opening many new doors for religious influence in all types of American colleges and universities. They need not be widely known but they must have the purpose and capacity to become colleges of educational excellence and of high religion.

In the three decades since World War I we have witnessed in other areas of education the revolutionary effects of such experiments. Many examples could be cited: the development of honors courses at Swarthmore; Antioch, with its alternation between work with books and work with hands, challenging the traditional conception of culture; Hiram, with its rearrangement of the school year and emphasis on intensive study of one thing at a time; Sarah Lawrence and Bennington, with their efforts to give a demonstration of the operation of the progressive educational philosophy in the higher education of women—to mention only a few. These were all either new creations or older colleges seized by a big idea and having the courage and capacity to carry it out. All of them have profoundly influenced the procedures of many colleges.

And now we are in the midst of other experiments—some of which come closer to the concern for more significant integration of religion with higher education. They deal with aims, content of curriculum, a better balance between the humanities and the natural sciences, the defining of a curriculum for general studies with an emphasis on core courses, the renewed interest in the classics, and a determination to do away with the evils of unlimited free election. At many of these points new experiments are being undertaken in which there is implicit, if not explicit, the desire to put every student in the possession of his cultural heritage, thus giving higher visibility to the spiritual forces that have shared in the shaping of our Western civilization.

It is too early to be sure, but from the evidence now at hand it would not appear that the church-related colleges are giving the aggressive leadership that society has a right to expect of them in this area of discovering new ways of integrating religion with the total life of the colleges. They do not seem to be doing *front-line fighting* in the battle against the secularism that has taken over our colleges as it has our society in the last three decades. There are too few colleges willing to bet their whole educational life on the finding of new ways of building Christian foundations for the total work of higher learning. Where are the colleges that will do the creative things in this area of religion that Swarthmore did three decades ago in honors course work? One of the tragedies is that many of the colleges that led in experiments in educational methods in the twenties have remained conservative and conventional in their approaches to religion in the life of the colleges.

There is a great deal of significant piecemeal experimentation going on in all types of colleges, including church-related colleges. Departments of religion are being strengthened and extended; exploration is being made of the new content for basic courses in religion; courses in religion are being drawn into core curricula; there is a new student wistfulness about religion; there has been a great increase in the number and quality of chaplains, Christian Association secretaries, and denominational workers in the colleges; educators in general, and administrators in particular, have been more outspoken in their advocacy and support of movements for strengthening religion among students; and there has been a strong revival of interest in the teaching of religion throughout the curriculum, making the religious perspectives of the various intellectual disciplines more visible. The sobering fact, however, is that one can call to mind as many state colleges as church-related colleges which are fired with zeal to build an educational experience that in its assumptions and processes supports a high view of religion. This is only an impression but, so far as it is correct, it is very disturbing.

All college administrators are agreed that the best way to guarantee an educational experience of religious significance is by increasing the number of faculty members who add to their scholarly distinction and skill as teachers the quality of a reasoned and contagious religious faith. The concern here is not for creedal affirmation, or church affiliation, but for the possession of a self-authenticating and inescapable religious faith. A state university president who felt limited because of legal restrictions in his support of religious instruction or movements pointed with pride to sixty new appointments he had made in ten years—most of which he sincerely believed had strengthened the concerns of religion in that great university. All of us can recall one or more professors who, in our undergraduate days, made a profound religious contribution to our lives because of what they were as persons, because of their high and noble enthusiasms, their devotion to truth, and the sense of comradeship which developed in their classrooms. They may never have said a word about religion or a "religious" word to us and yet the consequence was the strengthening of our religious faith. For more than a generation Professor William "Billy" Lyon Phelps exercised that kind of influence on thousands of Yale undergraduates.

The church-related college has a freedom in selection that is greater than that of any other institution. When a church college invites a professor to its staff it is asking him to share in the fellowship and work of a committed community. Whether the teacher is made aware of this fact is one of the questions raised in Dr. Espy's study of teachers in church-related colleges. The writer knows of no other recent study that is comparable to it in scholarly competence and significance. Because the problem is so central to the solution of all the other issues for religion in higher education, the book will be studied by all having a concern for strengthening religion in our American colleges. It is a model for thoroughness, objectivity in gathering data, and skill in interpretation.

In view of the widespread concern among educators in general it is surprising and disturbing to learn from this study that among these church college teachers "there is little evidence of profound intellectual wrestling with the problems of relationship between faith and fact, 'revealed' truth and scientific truth, religious method and educational method, religion and integrated curriculum." This and the fact that these teachers seem to get little help from their administrators in understanding the Christian objectives of these colleges would seem to support the suspicion stated above that, contrary to the reasonable expectations, the church-related colleges are not leaders in the new efforts to integrate religion and education. This is not to say that a similar study of the religion of teachers in private or state colleges would show any higher level of religious intelligence or concern for finding new ways. Perhaps also there is need for a study of those professors and administrators of church-related colleges who, as a minority group, do give evidence that they are doing new and fundamental thinking. But it is an occasion for both surprise and chagrin that on the whole the church colleges do not seem to be doing the front-line fighting.

In the reflection that this study gives of a "religious conformity which is approved by the community and the constituency of the college" the picture is also a disappointing one. One would have grounds for hoping to discover in the church-related colleges more of fresh, creative thinking on the nature of religion and the demands it makes on the individual, on education, and on society than one would expect to find elsewhere. One of the hopeful aspects of the study is its highlighting of the importance of graduate study in education and in religion as means for creating "greater maturity of religious faith, greater awareness of the relation of religious and educational values, and a greater readiness to disclose religious convictions in a manner consistent with sound educational process." According to the data, the same cannot be said for the courses in either education or religion at the undergraduate level.

The study throws much fresh light on the teacher's problems in counseling, his relation to the activities of the Christian Association and churches, his attitude towards his work as a Christian vocation, the time of decision and the influences leading to decision for teaching, and the periods of life in which the religious beliefs of these teachers—whether conservative or liberal—were formulated. Many of these professors work under such great pressure with their teaching and other academic responsibilities that few of them have had opportunity to develop their religious knowledge and convictions beyond the positions achieved when they were undergraduates. A task of religious education for the faculty confronts us today in all colleges, including those that are church-related.

The most important contribution of this study is the questions it raises concerning the prospects for religion in all colleges. The concern for closer integration of religion with higher education is still the possession of only a small minority of every faculty and perhaps of administrators. It will have to get down more fully into the ranks if its high hopes are to be realized.

CLARENCE PROUTY SHEDD

NEW HAVEN, CONN.
December, 1950

PREFACE

THE ORIGIN of this book is a doctoral dissertation on "The Religion of College Teachers" presented to the faculty of Yale University in May, 1950, in candidacy for the Ph.D. degree. The principal objective of the study was to secure and interpret facts not heretofore known on the views of teachers regarding the bearing of religion upon higher education.

Educationally, the relevance of religion to the purposes for which colleges and universities exist is increasingly acknowledged. This is especially true in liberal arts institutions, and above all in schools of whatever character which seek the enhancing of religious values as one of their educational aims. The central place of the teacher in relating religion to education also is widely recognized. The support of an institution's educational aims by the religious convictions of its teachers is an essential partnership for the difficult task of integrating religion and learning.

This study is concerned with religious values in higher education generally. It is confined to church-related colleges not because they are considered a more fertile field for the fusing of religious and educational insights than other institutions, but because for many reasons they presented a more accessible, cohesive, and compassable field for investigation. In any measure that the findings of this survey prove useful, they may encourage similar inquiries in other types of institutions. In the meantime, it is hoped that the results of the study will be relevant, if not fully applicable, to other colleges and universities than those related to churches.

Religiously, this book reflects the convergence of three concerns. First and foremost is a conviction concerning the lay membership of the Church, which includes college teachers. If we are to take Christianity seriously, we must come to grips with one of its clear demands—that all who profess that Christ is the Lord of their lives are called to make this manifest. The vitality of the Church, the chief organized expression of Christianity, will depend in the last analysis upon the vitality of its laymen, living the Christian life both within the churches and in the larger secular society. The Church must have laymen who conceive their life work, whatever it may be, as potentially a Christian vocation. What better place to examine the beliefs and practices of the layman than in the church-related college, where he may be presumed to have a favorable opportunity to express his Christian conviction?

A second religious concern is that of Christian unity. There is a growing realization that the work of the Church has suffered because of its divisions. In the language and activity of the Church, this concern for unity has found expression in the ecumenical movement, which seeks both to revitalize the life of the churches and to draw them closer together. In most of the church-related colleges, we have a Christian enterprise loyal to the denominations but seeking to transcend their differences and to develop a larger sense of unity and common purpose. While representing all the major streams of Protestantism, they represent also an ecumenical experience of long standing. An examination of the beliefs and practices of teachers in these institutions should provide data of ecumenical scope.

The third and more specific consideration prompting this study is the strategic importance of higher education in the fostering of religious values, and the particular role of the teacher in this objective. The significance of college teaching as an opportunity to impart a Christian outlook can not be overstated. It is a calling which can readily be regarded as a Christian vocation. The church-related colleges expect something of this motivation in their teachers. Certainly the communication of Christian insights in an educational institution is on an insecure foundation if it is not operative through the teachers. However much may be attempted through other desirable means, the role of the teacher will remain crucial and perhaps determinative. The teacher is a lay servant of the Church if he teaches in a church-related college. Hence the emphasis of this study upon the faculty member's concept of Christian vocation as it applies to his life work.

This book presents the views of a substantial number of teachers, selected on a random sampling basis. The views of a smaller group, who have given special thought to the integration of religion in their fields, is presented in the companion volume, *College Teaching and Christian Values*, edited by Dr. Paul M. Limbert. There one finds considered interpretations of college teaching as potentially a Christian vocation. Here we attempt to picture the present thinking and practice of the rank and file, and to point to possible ways in which the gap between the actual and the potential can be bridged.

While these concerns have provided the terms of reference for the book, the material has been gathered with no preconceptions as to what it would reveal. The writer is deeply indebted to the faculty members of Yale University who guided the inquiry on which the book is based. It was due to their supervision that the survey was conducted and interpreted on a sound research basis.

Special appreciation is expressed to Dean Emeritus Luther A. Weigle of the Yale University Divinity School, who assisted in the initial laying out of the project; to Professor Clyde M. Hill, head of the Graduate School of Education, whose desire to shape the study with a view to its practical usefulness provided constant stimulus and sense of direction; to Professor Clarence P. Shedd of the Divinity School, who was the chief instigator and unfailing inspirer of the enterprise from its earliest stages; and to Professor Hugh Hartshorne, whose painstaking and constructive advice on the preparation and distribution of the questionnaire was invaluable, and whose counsel on the organization of the manuscript helped the mass of raw data to come to life.

More than fifty persons, chiefly faculty members of Yale and other institutions both in America and abroad, made helpful suggestions on the preparation and circulation of the questionnaire. In addition, twenty teachers at Denison University, Maryville College, Oberlin College, and West Virginia Wesleyan College, with the encouragement of their presidents, served as test cases for a pilot study. To all of these persons and to the institutions they represent, we express sincere thanks.

Four organizations must be mentioned for their large part in the project. The generous action of the National Board of the Y.M.C.A. in releasing the writer for a year from most of his duties as Student Services secretary made the study possible. The National Protestant Council on Higher Education sponsored the project. Under the guidance of Dr. E. Fay Campbell, acting executive secretary, and Dr. Lawrence Foster, research consultant, the Protestant Council criticized the plans for the survey, enlisted the participation of the boards of education and the colleges, and helped organize the distribution of the questionnaires. The National Council on Religion in Higher Education also sponsored the study. On the initiative of the Reverend Seymour A. Smith, director, it provided channels to individuals who criticized the first formulation of the questionnaire and facilitated contact with some of the colleges in the survey. The Edward W. Hazen Foundation, under the leadership of Dr. Paul J. Braisted, president, offered help and encouragement in numerous ways, not least of which was the providing of ideal facilities and hospitality to the writer and his wife during the final six weeks of work on the dissertation.

Essential to all else was the participation of the teachers

themselves. Their readiness to wrestle with an intricate questionnaire, answering it fully and thoughtfully, is its own best
testimony to their concern and their spirit of co-operation.
The project is deeply in their debt for their indispensable
help. We trust that the results of their work as reflected in this
book will do them at least partial justice.

The book reorganizes, simplifies, and greatly condenses the
dissertation. It omits most of the tables, appendices, and technical statistics, while holding to its character as primarily a
book of research. The writer expresses heartfelt thanks to Professor Shedd, Dr. Campbell, and Dr. Lawrence K. Hall, director of Association Press, for their careful reading of the
manuscript in the revised form of the book, and for their helpful suggestions.

My profoundest gratitude is reserved for three persons
whose contribution to this study cannot be measured. Mrs. El-
mer A. Ansley spent more than a thousand hours in assisting me and my wife in tabulating replies, running comparisons, and typing and retyping the manuscript. The schedule she had to keep, along with her other commitments, was
more rigorous than most people would have been willing or
able to carry. Mr. John A. Antoinetti set aside other important matters to complete the statistical computations in time
to enable me to finish the dissertation by the deadline
date. Finally, it must be in the record that the study would
never have been begun, and certainly not completed by the
present time, except for the initial encouragement and the
tireless help of my wife, Cleo Mitchell Espy. She gave invaluable advice and countless hours of work on tabulations,
computations, proofreading, and other essential tasks. My indebtedness to her, to the others I have mentioned, and to
countless persons who must remain unnamed is deeper than
I can express.

R.H.E.E.

NEW YORK,
December, 1950

CONTENTS

TABLES

LIST OF APPENDICES

The Religion of College Teachers

1.

FACULTY VIEWPOINT: THE HEART OF HIGHER EDUCATION

How DO TEACHERS in the church-related colleges of the United States conceive and carry out their strategic role in education? What are their convictions concerning the distinctive functions of their institutions? Do they have a sense of Christian vocation in their life work?

The Setting

Only the teachers themselves can answer such questions authentically. Others can have opinions concerning the teachers' views, but their report must be second-hand. We shall try here to listen to the teachers. We desire to know what they think, not as an end in itself, but because the teacher is the key to education. We shall explore with them their viewpoints concerning the Christian import of the education which the church-related colleges and universities offer, and concerning their own part in this education.

The Protestant churches of America have made an honorable contribution to higher education. Our earliest institutions of higher learning were established under the stimulus of religious leadership, and were dedicated in large measure to the interests of "Church and Civil State." When public funds, through taxation or otherwise, were made available for the expanding enterprise of higher education, control by the churches was properly replaced in many emerging institutions by the authority of states and municipalities. But

1

the religious influence continued during the nineteenth century to impregnate the thinking of most of the leaders of our colleges and universities, regardless of the auspices or official connections of the particular institutions.

At the same time, the churches desired and needed colleges of their own which had full freedom to develop programs of higher education and which would give a central place to religion. They considered it important that Christian belief and practice should be propagated in the field of education as in all other areas of life. Religion should be made an integral part, they felt, of the intellectual development of young men and women. Christian education needed also to reach thousands of potential students, particularly on the expanding western frontiers, who otherwise would receive no college education of any kind. Under the impetus of these and closely related motives, church-related colleges multiplied in number, size, and influence. Their phenomenal growth is a familiar story.

Today, however, the historic functions of church-related institutions of higher education are often considered *passé*. Quite apart from the past, the question is pressed as to whether they have a valid contemporary function distinguishing them from other liberal arts colleges.

We must recognize that diversity is a hallmark of American higher education. From the time our earliest colleges were established, the founding of successive institutions has been on grounds not only of geography or population but of particularized objectives and functions. This has been especially true with the great growth in the number of such institutions since the first quarter of the nineteenth century. The resultant schools of higher learning do not exist for one commonly defined purpose but for many purposes, and represent widely varying educational outlooks.

The extensive current discussion of American higher education does not always differentiate among the types of institution being considered. Generalizations applying to the broad areas of common aim may be wide of the mark in relation to the more individualized objectives and needs of particular schools.

This study is concerned with colleges and universities related to Protestant churches. Some of the special aims of these institutions are not shared by other institutions. Without digressing here to analyze these distinctive aims, it is axiomatic that church-related colleges by very definition and connection are expected to help develop in students some of the Christian convictions, concepts, and character for which their respective supporting churches stand. The extent to which this broad objective is realized is a moot question. The current self-criticism on the part of church-related colleges is devoted, increasingly, to this issue.

Our special concern in this inquiry is the teacher. No examination of the impact of college education upon students and upon society can omit the well-nigh determinative influence of the teaching faculty. Except as the faculty member communicates the essential spirit of life and learning to which the institution is committed, all other efforts to reflect this spirit will necessarily be peripheral and only partially effective. This is particularly true in an institution which is concerned with values and with the growth of the whole person. It is significant that the theme of the 1950 meeting of the Association of American Colleges was "Great Teaching—the Essence of Liberal Education." If further evidence of the present concern for this issue were necessary, the numerous publications reflecting one or another phase of the problem provide ample substantiation.

The teacher is peculiarly central in an institution which calls itself Christian. It is a common-place that religious faith and its meanings for life are best communicated through persons. But do the persons whose influence upon students is greatest, the teachers themselves, consider their task in its religious bearings? How do the teachers conceive their role, if at all, as mediators of a Christian philosophy of life? Teachers and administrators alike should know the climate of faculty opinion on this basic issue of Christian higher education.

The Problem

Before seeking to answer these questions, we must state an assumption which underlies them. It is the assumption which is inherent in the Christian faith and life—that every man, as a child of God, has a role to play in God's will for the world. Whether he be priest or prince, savant or yokel, gardener or statesman, he is answerable before the universe for what he does with his life. He can not escape the question of life vocation, for life has to be lived, and every phase of it is related in some inscrutable way to the divine purpose. In particular, what he does to earn his daily bread can become a testimony of faith and an instrument of God's work in the world. Every honorable occupation can be made a Christian calling.

This is what it means to be a Christian layman. The Christian mission in the world involves every member of the Church, regardless of how inclusively the Church may be conceived. In any measure that there is a priesthood of all believers, there is a universality of Christian vocation. Just as all are imbued by the Creator with the sacredness of human personality, so all are responsible to the Creator as the source of their sacredness. Clergy and laity alike are called through their respective fields of work to help fulfill God's purposes in their own lives and in society.

This is strange language to the prevailing modern mind. It is a truism that life in the twentieth century is highly secularized. In its simplest but profoundest terms, secularism is the living of life apart from a consciousness of God. Not only in the complex decisions affecting our society as a whole, where the relevance of God may be hard to see, but in the individual decisions directly related to our personal lives, we act as if man were on his own. Those who are faithful to certain religious observances often appear as little concerned for the will of God in their daily actions as are those who profess no religious faith. There is a yawning chasm between our reverence at church and our reverence at the shop or lectern.

One of the places where the churches of the United States have sought to bridge this gap through lay leadership is in their colleges and universities. Here the Church and the world come together. The Protestant denominations have not sought to obliterate the differences nor to eradicate the problem, for they know that the tension of living in the world but not of it is part of the reality of the Christian life. Living in this tension also is the means of Christian witness. Thus the church-related colleges have sought to be neither religious monasteries nor academic ivory towers. One of their cardinal strengths is their confrontation with life. Through them, the churches have sought at a strategic point to speak in and to the world.

The question remains, however, as to how incisively the churches and the colleges have articulated their distinctive task in higher education. In particular, it is questionable to what extent clear concepts in this regard have been communicated to the teachers, and to what extent the teachers find the concepts acceptable. It is frequently stated that teachers chafe under the "restrictions" of church-related colleges. Do either the teachers, the administrations, or the churches have a philosophy of religion in higher education which transcends the purely restrictive and promulgates a noble and sweeping view of college education with God at its center?

Generalizations concerning the religious views of college teachers are, of course, frequently voiced. So also are philosophical or theological formulations of what these views

ought to be in the interest of sound Christian higher education. Largely lacking up to now has been an analysis of the
actual views of the teachers, who are not only the strategic
persons in the educational process but are the persons best
qualified to say what the teachers think and do in these
areas.

The objective of this study has been to secure and interpret
first-hand evidence from the expressions of teachers themselves. It seeks to examine especially their own religious beliefs and practices in relation to their life work as teachers,
and to draw them out on possible measures for the better
training of future teachers for the church-related colleges.

The Data

Our attempt to discover teachers' views on these questions
has been confined to undergraduate, four-year colleges of
Protestant connection. It includes no teachers of religion,
seeking rather a cross-section of the views and activities of
teachers in other subject-matter fields. Depending upon the
teacher, these fields might or might not be construed as having
a religious bearing.

To provide a sampling from the three major areas of the
humanities, the physical sciences, and the social sciences, the
inquiry was addressed to teachers of English, physics, and
sociology-economics. The last two subjects were bracketed
together as one, because many teachers in the smaller institutions are related to both. In the analysis of the replies, the
teachers were regarded as representing four fields.

The study does not attempt, however, to analyze issues concerning the relation of religion to a particular subject matter
per se. It examines, rather, the teacher's broad philosophy
and practice regarding the relation of his religion to his professional responsibility. It deals both with his teaching, including its many attendant tasks, and with his extracurricular
relationships to students and in the institution as a whole.

After considering a number of plans for securing the teachers' views, the method decided upon was the circulation of an extensive questionnaire. A condensation of the instrument employed is included as Appendix I of this book. Appendix II describes briefly the procedure adopted in distributing the questionnaire and the methods employed in interpreting the data received.

Despite our reliance upon numbers and percentages as the source of our findings, this is not to be considered as primarily a statistical study. The field of opinion does not lend itself readily to exact statistical formulations where the subject matter is as elusive as is that of religious belief. This study is an interpretive survey which has used statistics in so far as they could be used responsibly. It has attempted to avoid generalizations and to draw only such wider inferences from the data as the evidence justifies.

Sixty per cent of the teachers who received questionnaires filled out and returned them. Of this number, four hundred forty were adjudged valid for inclusion in the study. They represented seventy-three colleges of twenty-nine denominations, only one denomination on the original list failing to be included. The colleges were well distributed as to geography, size, race, co-education, type of accreditation, and other criteria. This is indicated in Appendix III.

The individual teachers were well distributed as to subjects taught, faculty status, academic degrees, denominational affiliation, sex, and type of undergraduate institution from which they had graduated. Their representativeness is suggested by Table I.

Emergent Issues

We are concerned with the viewpoint of the teacher not only because it is the key to understanding a college, but because the faculty is the principal source of impact upon a college. The teacher is the heart of higher education. To

TABLE I

DISTRIBUTION OF THE 440 TEACHERS

	Number	Per cent
Subjects taught:		
English	210	48
Sociology	76	17
Economics	79	18
Physics	75	17
Total	440	100%
Faculty status:		
Deans (incl. 2 presidents)	16	4
Department heads	29	7
Professors	147	33
Associate professors	63	14
Assistant professors	105	24
Instructors	80	18
Total	440	100%
Academic degrees:		
Ph.D. degree and other doctoral degrees	155	35
B.D. and other theological degrees	15	3
Master's degree, but no higher degree	236	54
No degree above the bachelor's	34	8
Total	440	100%
Denominations represented	34	
Geographical areas represented:		
Middle States	75	17
North Central	203	46
Southern	124	28
Northwest	38	9
Total	440	100%
Type of undergraduate institution from which teacher graduated:		
Church-related	254	58
Public (State, Municipal, etc.)	118	27
Independent, non-church-related	68	15
Total	440	100%
Division of teachers according to sex:		
Men	331	75
Women	109	25
Total	440	100%

have in hand the frank and unstinted opinions of 440 college teachers concerning their religious outlook and its bearing on their work as teachers is a peculiar privilege which could easily be abused. How is it possible to represent these teachers fairly?

It must be seen at the outset that no interpretation of the views of so varied a group can do them justice. This is particularly obvious in an area as intangible as that embraced by this study. Only the generous participation of the teachers themselves, who not only filled out a lengthy questionnaire, but ninety per cent of whom volunteered their own additional interpretations, generates the confidence to attempt this accounting of their views. There is encouragement, too, in the fact that the teachers have requested a report on their self-evaluations. They are the first to recognize that the faculty viewpoint is determinative in higher education, and they are eager to know the opinions of their colleagues in sister institutions.

The issues emerging from the teachers' replies and comments run the full gamut of church-related higher education. Any college president, trustee, or board of education secretary may be assured on the basis of these data that his problems, whatever they may be, have had the thinking of some college teacher. Indeed, numerous comments would suggest that the teachers feel that they are closer to the problems than are their administrative superiors.

Both the intellectual issues and the practical problems are recognized by the teachers as highly complex. Most of them show no sense of restraint in speaking frankly about those in authority, but they are equally frank with themselves. Their replies to questions and their supplementary comments are earnest, and give evidence for the most part of careful consideration. Many realize that they have conceived their Christian responsibility as teachers within the narrow limits of their personal Christian character and example rather than relating it to their work as teachers; they express a new concern for the integration of their religious beliefs with their intellectual disciplines and teaching practices. Others see little relationship between their religion and their teaching. All have suggestions regarding the more adequate preparation they feel is needed for Christian college teachers of the future.

We shall not anticipate the teachers' viewpoints here. Let us note, however, the several categories into which their answers and observations divide. The first, presented in Chapter 2, comprises background information providing a composite picture of the teachers. We examine their reasons for deciding to enter this life work, and the timing of their decisions; the extent and character of the academic training with which they equipped themselves; the nature and scope of their present responsibilities, both academic and extra-curricular; and the degree to which they are growing on their jobs, both through formal in-service training and through more individualized discipline.

We consider next the more specific religious material, comprising Chapter 3. We shall find that the issues here embrace the following major questions: What leadership do the teachers give in relation to their churches? What are their basic religious beliefs, and what is the nature of their religious life? How, if at all, do they relate their religious concepts to their educational concepts? to their particular subject matter fields? to their teaching practices, notably the problem of disclosing or not disclosing their religious beliefs in the class-room? to their personal contacts with students and student activities? to their participation in the life of the college as a whole? to social issues? On all of these questions the teachers' views are varied. We shall attempt to delineate broad directions of agreement, while taking full account of minorities.

The securing of the teachers' opinions on these issues is

of only partial value in itself. Of equal importance is their judgment regarding training and other factors which were determinative in the development of these views. In Chapter 4, therefore, we ask the teachers for their own analysis of their training and we make a corollary analysis by comparison of particular concepts and practices with particular background factors. We analyze the periods and the academic influences, if any, to which the formulation of certain views can be traced; we look for correlations between religious beliefs and denominational affiliations; we examine the similarities and differences of teachers who attended different types of undergraduate colleges; we consider the effects of geographical location, faculty status, and subject-matter fields. In particular, we explore the influence exerted upon the teachers' views by their academic training, and we analyze the teachers' self-evaluation of their preparation for teaching. These data reveal some of the possibilities for improvement of future training.

In the concluding chapter we shall attempt to draw together the principal findings of the foregoing data, and to state some major issues for the future. An effort is made to formulate these problems functionally, in the sense that every issue stated poses a question as to what should be *done*. There is ample provocation in the data of Chapters 3 and 4 for extended discussion of theological issues and educational principles. These problems are basic and inescapable, and the posing of functional issues does not seek to evade them; but the functional approach may have more practical and immediate value than intellectual debate in isolating the issues which call for decisions of policy and strategy among the leaders of Christian higher education, including the teachers themselves.

The underlying question is the one with which we began: whether the teachers truly comprehend and seek to carry out their strategic Christian role as the principal source of influence upon the students. Do they have and disclose a sense of Christian vocation in their life work as teachers in church-related colleges? To provide a setting for their answers, the following chapter presents a composite picture of the teachers themselves.

2.

FACULTY PROFILE:
THE COMPOSITE TEACHER

WE HAVE NOTED the broad representativeness of the responding teachers in terms of subjects taught, faculty status, academic degrees, denominational affiliation of their colleges, geographical location, and the types of institutions in which they received their undergraduate training. It is not intended at this stage to advance particular theses concerning the teachers studied nor concerning the larger group they represent, but rather to furnish factual background for subsequent interpretation. The relevance of these facts to the college teacher's religion may not be immediately apparent, but they are necessary for orientation and for an understanding of our later analysis.

The Decision to Teach

Present life attitudes often are determined by early influences and decisions. What were the inner reasons of the faculty members in this survey for deciding to become college teachers? The motivations mentioned by half or more of the respondents are the following: "you felt that you would enjoy teaching as such," 80 per cent; "you desired to work with college students," 78 per cent; "you were primarily interested in the subject matter," 66 per cent; "you wanted to add to the body of human knowledge," 55 per cent; "you

13

regarded college teaching as a strategic Christian vocation," 50 per cent.

The commanding lead accorded the four attractions of teaching which are distinctly academic is to be expected. That half of the teachers mention the conception of college teaching as a strategic Christian vocation will be interpreted later. The offer of an actual teaching position and the prestige, security, and associations of college life were further determinative factors in the decisions of two-fifths of the teachers. Any college presidents who are fearful of faculty competition for their posts may be reassured to know that only one out of twenty of their teachers entered the profession with the thought of moving into college administration!

One-sixth of the responses specify "other" reasons for becoming college teachers. Some of these we shall quote. One teacher asserts that he "never noticed any particular prestige or security in connection with it, by comparison with other professional occupations." In contrast, another says that his parents, who "are not graduates of any school, were impressed by the prestige it would give them" for their son to be a teacher, and that this was a major reason for his decision.

This difference of viewpoint concerning prestige raises an important question which is considered by the President's Commission on Higher Education. Discussing inducements to teaching, it deals with salaries, tenure, and provisions for retirement. It then states, "Beyond these factors, the most important aid in enlisting and recruiting teachers is psychological. In a national poll conducted for the Commission, college professors rank seventh in a rating of the prestige of ninety occupations, topped only by United States Supreme Court justices, physicians, state governors, members of the President's cabinet, diplomats in the United States foreign service, and mayors of large cities. It is apparent that teaching in college is generally recognized as one of the most important services to society, but too few young people are aware of this fact."[1]

Apart from medicine, the occupations here listed are much more highly specialized than college teaching in the sense that they do not claim nearly as many persons. Of the callings involving large numbers, it would appear that the college teacher stands next to the doctor in public esteem.

Some teachers chose this vocation because of their dissatisfaction with its present practitioners. One person, a Ph. D. and professor, says, "I was attracted to teaching because I felt I could do a better job of it than some of my teachers!" Another cites the "poor quality of most of the college teaching I came in contact with" as a reason for entering the field.

A large number of the teachers giving "other" reasons simply provide variations on the theme of the intellectual attractions of college life. Selecting some examples with amusing import, we find a teacher fortifying his profession of intellectual concern with the report that he was a formidable chess player—in fact, one-time captain of the Stanford chess team! Another first recognized his capacities when he "made the highest grade in class." One teacher appears to identify the good life of the mind with the life of minimum effort, college teaching being "about the only easily attainable way of life that leaves room for intellectual pursuits."

Six teachers, in addition to those checking prestige and security, stress the economic motive, though a much larger number express distress at their personal economic plight and that of their colleges. In the main, the number of persons who are college teachers despite the economic factor appears far

---

[1] *Higher Education for American Democracy*, a Report by The President's Commission on Higher Education. New York: Harper and Brothers, 1948. Vol. IV, p. 28.

greater than the number who chose it for economic advantage.

Among the transfers from business to the college field, one teacher mentions "dissatisfaction of soul in industry; illness made me reflect and change my goal." There are an indeterminable but substantial number of teachers who at one time were ministers. The reasons for the transfer of members of this group to college teaching are related in the main to intellectual attractions, but one explanation is too revealing to be omitted. This ex-minister writes, "I changed to teaching because it was easier on my wife!"

Nearly half of the teachers listing "other" factors cite service motives, ranging from one who stresses his sense of "cultural vocation" to one who states, "I was convinced of divine guidance toward this field of service." The dean of one of the colleges says, "Like many a young soldier, I decided I could do most where I could talk most freely. I wanted to be a propagandist for better human relations."

Two comments give teaching a comparative ranking with other callings as an avenue of service. One says, "I felt that next to preaching, it was the greatest service profession." Another regards "teaching as second only to agriculture in its fundamental value to society."

A professor of economics, born and trained in Europe, considered college teaching the best outlet for his capacities and the best means "to bring to bear my cultural Judaeo-Christian heritage." For the English teachers, a spokesman states, "I believe that literature offers the best synthesis of life—for soul and body, material and immaterial—in the liberal arts college."

We conclude these random quotations with the comment of a teacher of physics: "As far as I know, this profession offers the only opportunity—outside of a private income—for a conscientious man to develop 'freely' with a minimum of constraints upon his beliefs and practices. It is a 'way of life' which we once thought was necessary in order to develop in our society a small group of objective critics. Free discussion with the open minds of young people is an important ingredient. So is economic security, though today non-existent."

Thus the reasons for becoming college teachers are legion. So also are the influences in the form of persons. There is clear evidence that teachers are produced primarily by teachers. Naming the categories of people who pointed them toward college teaching, 62 per cent mentioned their professors. Two-thirds of this group credit two or more professors with a decisive influence, while one-third cited one professor. Parents were not quite half as high as the total for professors.

The influence of specifically religious leadership or religious programs falls relatively low, with a total of one-fifth of the teachers mentioning one of the four categories of minister, student religious worker, Student Christian Movement program, or denominational student program. After adjustment for overlappings, only 14 per cent of the respondents are represented in this multiple-choice total, the highest percentage for a single item being 7 per cent for ministers. Some of the respondents go out of their way to bracket these four items and to state that they were not influenced by any one of them. One teacher reflects that it is "possibly significant that none of these reasons (the four involving religious leadership or program) had any possible influence that I can recall." Another commentator stresses the negative effect of his minister's influence, which he had to overcome in college before deciding to become a college teacher.

A fourth of the teachers mention "other" influences. Leading this list are 4 per cent of the 440 citing a college president, and another 4 per cent referring to members of their family other than parents, chiefly persons who were themselves teachers. They include uncles, brothers, cousins, wives, husbands, and grandfathers. One professor turns genealogical, stating that his "ancestors had been teachers since 1579 at least, possibly longer." Still another 4 per cent mention different categories of "friends," chiefly college teachers other than their own professors. One, acknowledging no direct influence through a personal association, cites the intellectual influence of "Montaigne, Rabelais, Plato, Emerson, Newman, Tyndall, Huxley, Jeans, and a fairly long tradition of the University."

The failure of many respondents to mention any personal associations in response to this question leads to a final observation regarding the teachers' attitude toward personal influence upon their vocational decisions. One-tenth of them are at pains to disavow any such influence. They appear to take pride in having decided for themselves. A number put the word "influence" in quotes and carefully proscribe it, as if it were dishonorable. We frequently meet such statements or phrases as "I don't think external factors played an important part in my choice;" "I was not 'influenced' by any one;" "pretty much my own decision, without outside influence;" "made up my own mind;" "my own individual desire;" "my own choice;" "my own inclination;" "strictly by my own desire;" "entirely of my own choice and decision;" "my own wishes;" "my own judgment;" "independent decision;" "myself;" "no person or organization influenced me."

These declarations of independence suggest a subtle defensiveness on the part of the teachers involved. The factor of influence by other persons evidently has a negative connotation in their minds. It would be quite understandable for a considerable proportion of the teachers to report that they did not recall who influenced them most, or that they could not distinguish such persons within the categories suggested. But it is scarcely conceivable that no person contributed to their desire to become college teachers; and to insist that they have been influenced by no one suggests a certain lack of objective realism as well as of personal sense of indebtedness.

Turning to chronology, the reason for deciding to become a college teacher can not be dissociated from the timing of the decision. There is a note of wistfulness in the fact that all except one of the 440 teachers answered the question on timing, and that more than a fourth of them mentioned special periods or circumstances associated with their decision. The following breakdown into major periods or environing factors is worthy of note:

TABLE II

PERIODS OF DECISION TO BECOME COLLEGE TEACHERS

	% of Teachers
As an undergraduate	33
During graduate training	27
Before entering college	14
While teacher or administrator in a high school	7
Between college and graduate work	4
At other times and under other circumstances	15
Total	100%

It is clear that the two distinctly academic periods, with a total of 60 per cent, predominate. Most of the persons who designate the precollege period are in the group who cited their parents as a major influence. The number who transferred from high school work is high, and may be even higher than here suggested, as some teachers indicating in other connections that they had taught in high school do not state this fact here. A number attribute their decision to experience in the armed services, during one or the other of the World Wars. An additional teacher, a pacifist, was in Civilian Public Service and then in prison as a non-registrant during World War II. He writes that this experience influenced him, "though I might well have made a similar decision in the absence of these facts."

It is plain from these disclosures that the inner reasons for deciding to become college teachers are as numerous and varied as are the teachers themselves. It is also clear that the

major personal influence was that of respected teachers, and
that the major period for such decisions was that of college
or graduate study. The motivations for the most part were
of the highest. The reader may judge for himself whether
the 50 per cent who entered college teaching partly because
they considered it a strategic Christian vocation is a poor
showing or a good one. We shall note in Chapter 4 that a
larger number of these same teachers would consider this
factor if they were making the decision today.

Academic Training

Though most of the teachers had completed a considerable
part of their academic work before they knew what their life
vocation was to be, their training both before and after this
decision was made is of great importance. We can sketch only
those training factors which have a particular bearing on the
central concern of this study.

In contrast to the practice in many European universities,
three-fourths of our 440 teachers attended only one undergraduate institution. Four-fifths of them were awarded B. A.
degrees and one-sixth B. S. degrees, while the small remaining number received other degrees. They attended 248 undergraduate institutions, and are now located in the same
geographical areas, generally speaking, as those in which
they did their undergraduate training.

Fifty-eight per cent of the teachers received their undergraduate degrees from church-related colleges or universities, 27 per cent from public-supported institutions, and 15
per cent from independent, non-church-related schools. We
shall examine later the extent to which these differences of
background appear to have a bearing on the teachers' religious concepts and practices in relation to their teaching.

Regarding undergraduate courses in religion, 23 per cent
had no such courses, 44 per cent had from one to ten hours,
averaging approximately six hours, and 19 per cent had

eleven hours or over. This does not include those whose answers were unclear or who did not reply.

The teachers were asked how much undergraduate work they had had in education: "courses in the philosophy, history, theory, psychology or method of education." Only one-fourth of the teachers answering the question stated definitely that they had had no such courses but some who report courses in education appear to have confused education courses with other courses. We find also a manifest antipathy on the part of many of the teachers toward education courses. One of them avails himself of the opportunity as follows: "I take you at your word here and answer 'none' if you mean the 'education' courses dear to the hearts of teachers' colleges. My own belief is that *any* course under a good teacher is an education course."

Another professor answers, "A good many. But I think two semester courses enough for the ordinary professor. He should, however, have a good deal of psychology, philosophy, sociology, history, etc." An outspoken Ph.D. replies, "I do not think education courses have any value whatever except for mediocre persons, who probably shouldn't be teaching anyway!"

As we shall see later, a check of the concepts and practices of the quarter of the teachers who indicate that they did not take any undergraduate education courses discloses no significant differences in their educational or religious attitudes from those of the rest of the teachers. Similarly, there is no evidence of a consistent effect exerted upon these attitudes by courses in practice teaching.

Turning to graduate education, it is perhaps surprising to find our teachers attending in the aggregate nearly as many separate institutions after graduation as they did undergraduate institutions. A total of 196 institutions for graduate study were attended, and the separate attendances for graduate study totalled 910, or an average of 2.1 per teacher.

One clue to the wide variety of schools attended after graduation is that the church-related connections of both the undergraduate schools attended and the schools where the teachers are now serving undoubtedly caused many to take graduate work at the smaller institutions related to churches. Thus, of the 196 institutions, fifty-eight are church-related; but they record only ninety-four, or 10 per cent, of the 910 total attendances at graduate institutions. These attendances are divided among seventy-six teachers, or only 17 per cent of the total 440. This is in contrast to the 58 per cent of the teachers who did their undergraduate work at church-related institutions. We must further note that many of the church-related institutions attended for graduate work are, strictly speaking, not graduate schools.

Not only do the teachers take relatively little of their graduate study in church-related institutions, but three-fourths of those who do attend these institutions are graduates of church-related colleges. The traffic from non-church-related undergraduate schools as a whole to church-related graduate schools is significantly lighter than that from the church-related institutions.[2]

The totals we have cited include the large proportion of teachers attending theological or other religious training schools. Of the fifty-eight institutions, thirty-one are of this character. Of the seventy-six persons involved, thirty-nine studied largely in this type of school, including interdenom-

---

[2] $CR = 2.84$; $P = .005$.

Selected statistical results of this study will be recorded in footnotes where deemed desirable for a fuller understanding of the data. In accordance with the character of the particular statistics, the tests of Chi-square and/or Critical Ratio were applied to the most important tables. The .05 level of significance was used ($P = .05$), *i.e.*, the results obtained could have occurred by chance less than five times in one hundred. A critical ratio figure of 1.96 corresponds to the .05 level of significance. Generally, 1.96 was used as the index of significance throughout the interpretation.

inational religious training schools. Thus there remain only thirty-seven teachers, or 8 per cent of the total, who did other than religious courses at church-related graduate schools.

Before proceeding to the broader picture of overall graduate training, it is important as background for later analysis that we sketch a profile of the thirty-nine teachers, or 9 per cent of the total, who did a year or more of graduate work in the field of religion. Most of this group of teachers had considerably more than one year of such work.

It is significant for our study that this large a proportion of the 440 teachers had substantial graduate study in religion. The colleges involved evidently encourage, in addition to credit courses in religion and general religious orientation on the part of faculty members in all fields, the placing in some departments of certain teachers who have had specialized training in religion beyond their preparation in their own academic disciplines.

The fact that this many of the teachers felt the need of special training in religion as an aid to their teaching in other fields says something also about the teachers themselves, for the great majority of this group did not drift from the ministry or other religious work into teaching, but made the decision before or during their academic training and moved direct from graduate work into teaching. They took intensive work in religion because they felt it would help them in teaching sociology, English, economics, or even physics. By far the largest proportion are teaching sociology, approximately one-third of the sociologists in the survey having taken specialized work in religion. Six per cent of the English teachers had such training, and one teacher each in economics and physics.

These thirty-nine teachers are representative of the teachers as a whole in geographical location, faculty status, graduate degrees received, denominational affiliation, and the denominational connection of the colleges where they are teaching. It is of interest, however, that three-quarters of them had attended church-related undergraduate institutions.

The thirty-nine teachers took their graduate study in religion in thirty-one different institutions. This is a commentary on the number of such schools available, the wide diversity of offerings in the field, and the improbability that any one theological viewpoint is inundating the unsuspecting classrooms of our church-related colleges!

An additional 6 per cent of the 440 teachers had some, but very little, graduate work in religion. Half of this group report only one to three hours, a third report from four to six hours, and a sixth report ten hours or above. Thus of the total of 15 per cent of the teachers with any graduate work in religion, the amount taken by at least a third of them may be characterized as a negligible graduate training in religion.

The number of graduate courses in education is higher. One-third of the teachers specifically cite such courses. Twenty per cent had from one to ten hours, 14 per cent had eleven hours or more, and an additional 2 per cent had what apparently was full work in education for a minimum of a year, in some cases considerably longer. Later analysis will indicate some of the special viewpoints and contributions of the group of teachers with special graduate work in education, as well as of the group with special graduate work in religion.

We are brought now from the consideration of graduate study in these special fields to the area of graduate study as a whole. The average which we have noted of 2.1 graduate school attendances for each of the 440 teachers represents an average attendance of 4.6 persons at each of the 196 institutions. There is thus much greater movement of individual students from one institution to another in graduate work than was the case with undergraduates. Only 2 per cent of the teachers have done no graduate work, while 37 per cent have studied in one graduate school, 33 per cent have studied in two, 17 per cent have studied in three, and 11 per cent have studied in four or more. The number of years they have spent in graduate study ranges from none for the 2 per cent without graduate study to as high as ten years, with a fairly even spread of percentages from one to four years. Approximately one-fifth report respectively one year, two years, three years, and four years each, while one-tenth report five years and one-tenth report six years or more.

The graduate degrees received would merit detailed special study, if this were our particular task. We have noted the broad percentages in the preceding chapter. These figures correspond closely with prevailing ratios in church-related colleges.

With respect to the Ph. D., we are able to compare our spread of degrees with that of teachers in higher education generally. According to the President's Commission, our proportions are again closely in line. "In 1945 a survey of 305 fairly strong colleges and universities revealed that in 10 per cent of the institutions, . . . the median institution would be one with less than 35 per cent of its teaching staff holding that (the Ph. D.) degree."[3] We find that our holders of Ph. D.'s (and nine other doctoral degrees), representing 35.22 per cent of our sampling, correspond to the fifty-second percentile as charted by the President's Commission in a ranking of institutions by percentiles of one to one hundred. Thus the ratio of doctoral degrees to the total number of teachers in our study is remarkably close to the ratio cited by the President's Commission for "fairly strong colleges" as a whole.

When, on the whole, do the teachers do their graduate work? Is it chiefly before or after they start their college

---

[3] *Op. cit.*, Vol. IV, pp. 4-5.

teaching? Allowing for ambiguities, especially with respect to the twilight zone of teaching fellowships and instructorships while studying, the replies indicate that 71 per cent of the master's degrees, 69 per cent of the B. D. and other theological degrees, and 28 per cent of the doctoral degrees are secured before starting to teach.

A further breakdown of the master's degrees reveals that the M. S. usually is obtained later than the M. A., only 57 per cent of the teachers with the M. S. receiving the degree before they start teaching, as against 74 per cent for the holders of the M. A. degree. It is also of interest that 14 per cent of all the teachers took no graduate work before they started teaching, and 31 per cent have taken no graduate work since they started teaching.

Two-fifths of the teachers in our study are serving in colleges of the same denominations as the ones they attended as undergraduates. One-fourth of the teachers are serving in the same schools where they had all or part of their own undergraduate training. The tendency in this direction appears to be strongest in some of the Lutheran institutions and in institutions of several smaller denominations.

The majority of the 910 separate attendances for graduate study is concentrated on a relatively small number of institutions. Thus 608 of these attendances were in only twenty-eight institutions. This is seen in Table III, which also shows the number of degrees conferred on those of our teachers who attended these graduate schools.

This record represents an average of 1.38 attendances for each of the 440 teachers at the schools listed. Four-fifths of the total doctoral degrees were earned in these institutions. We shall note later some of the factors which caused the teachers to do their graduate work where they did.

The location in the Midwest of the preponderance of institutions attended for graduate study is probably to be expected. Their central geographical position for the country

TABLE III

INSTITUTIONS IN WHICH THE LARGEST NUMBER
OF TEACHERS HAVE DONE GRADUATE WORK

Institutions	No. of Teachers' Separate Attendances	% of 440 Teachers Attending Institutions	No. of Graduate Degrees	
			Doctoral	Others
University of Chicago	101	23	14	40
Columbia University	53	12	3	18
University of Wisconsin	40	9	6	21
Harvard University	36	8	8	23
University of Michigan	35	8	4	20
University of Minnesota	26	6	4	5
Ohio State University	25	6	9	11
State University of Iowa	24	5	7	12
Northwestern University	23	5	3	13
University of Pennsylvania	22	5	6	14
University of North Carolina	19	4	9	6
University of Washington	17	4	4	11
University of California	16	4	4	3
University of Illinois	14	3	3	9
University of Southern California	14	3	2	3
Cornell University	13	3	5	2
University of Virginia	13	3	7	6
University of Pittsburgh	12	3	2	9
Yale University	12	3	8	2
Duke University	11	3	2	6
Johns Hopkins University	11	3	1	4
New York University	11	3	2	6
George Peabody College for Teachers	10	2	2	4
Indiana University	10	2	3	2
University of Missouri	10	2	2	6
Oxford University	10	2	—	4
Syracuse University	10	2	—	7
University of Texas	10	2	3	6
Totals	608	138	123	273

as a whole, their great size and capacity to absorb students, and the location of 46 per cent of our responding teachers in the extensive North Central area might in themselves account for this concentration. On the other side, these considerations, combined with the fact that none of the seventy-three schools in our survey is located in New England, make it worthy of note that we find as large a proportion of the teachers as we do who are taking graduate work as far east as Columbia, Harvard, Pennsylvania, Yale, Johns Hopkins, New York University, and Syracuse.

This completes our teacher profile on academic training. We have noted an unclear record on undergraduate courses in education, an uneven record in undergraduate religion courses, a fair but varied background of graduate study in education, and on the whole a meager graduate training in religion. On the other hand, the average amount of total graduate work is high, the number of doctoral degrees is slightly above the average for teachers in comparable institutions, and there is a strong concentration of graduate experience in institutions of high grade. We shall now examine briefly the teachers' background of previous professional experience and the character of their present duties.

Teacher at Work

Teaching experience ranges from a fraction of a year in the cases of two of our teachers to forty-one years or over in the cases of two others. One-third of the teachers entered the profession during the five years from 1944 to 1948, one-sixth had entered during the previous five years, one-fifth have been teaching eleven to twenty years, the same number from twenty-one to thirty years, and the remaining tenth have been teaching thirty-one years or more. There is thus a reassuring balance between youth and venerability in these college faculties. Dividing the group differently, half have been teaching from one to ten years, and half for more than ten years.

But what of stability in relation to a particular institution? Is there a tendency to migrate in search of greener pastures? The fact that 35 per cent have had no previous teaching position, 29 per cent have had one previous position, and 19 per cent have had two previous positions, is a reliable index. Only 17 per cent, including 3 per cent who gave no clear answer, have changed positions as many as three times. This is despite the fact that 50 per cent of the teachers have been in the profession over ten years.

In terms not necessarily of the college or university where the teacher is now serving, but of church-related institutions as a whole, our teachers appear satisfied with their locations. A slight majority desired before they began teaching to teach in a particular type of institution, preferably in most cases in a church-related college. In response to the question, "Are you teaching in the type of institution you now prefer?" 86 per cent say yes and only 10 per cent say no. Whether this is a commentary on the attractions of the institutions or on the docility of the teachers, we do not as yet presume to judge. Whatever the reasons, the great majority of the teachers appear to be happy professionally in church-related colleges.

This favorable report conforms with the views of college teachers generally concerning their work. Thus the President's Commission states, on the basis of its 1946-47 survey of twenty-nine institutions, " . . . morale of college faculties was not low. . . . Four out of five wanted to stay with their particular college, and nine out of ten wanted to remain in college teaching. These attitudes are borne out also by a similar study conducted for the Commission by the American Association of University Professors."[4]

Three-fourths of the teachers are teaching the subjects they originally expected to teach, and the majority of the remainder have changed by desire, with the result that they are now teaching what they want to teach. One-fourth of those who have changed did so because they developed a preference for their present field; one-tenth because they were attracted by the greater social significance of the present field; 7 per cent because of its greater religious significance; 5 per cent because of their greater competence in the present field; 4 per cent because they are now able to reach more students; and

[4] *Op. cit.*, Vol. IV, p. 49.

2 per cent because they felt a greater need for teachers in the present field. On the other side, the more desultory reasons for change are in the minority: because an opening was offered; because there are more openings generally in the field; or because the teacher was unable to get the desired training in the original field. In short, there is general present satisfaction not only with the type of institution but with the field of teaching.

On the other hand, the data clearly reveal that the widespread complaint of teachers in church-related colleges concerning their overload of work is grounded in ineluctable fact. Concerning the teaching load itself, the reports show 35 per cent of the teachers carrying from eleven to fourteen hours weekly, 35 per cent carrying fifteen hours, and 19 per cent sixteen hours or above. The schedule of concomitant academic duties adds substantial responsibility beyond actual teaching. Thus research and laboratory work, preparation of lectures, reading of papers, academic counseling of students, and other responsibilities related directly to teaching require sixteen to twenty hours for 14 per cent of the respondents; twenty-one to thirty hours for 32 per cent; thirty-one to forty hours for 21 per cent; and forty-one to fifty hours for 10 per cent. Of the remaining 23 per cent, approximately one-third spend over fifty hours in these duties. Fortunately, an analysis of individual questionnaires reveals that the heaviest loads in teaching and in the auxiliary academic duties usually do not fall on the same person.

But there is difficulty in an area less directly related to teaching. It appears to be expected in most of the colleges under study that the teacher's "free" hours are to be utilized for other good works. The heaviest concentration here is about equally divided among:

1. Non-academic counseling, either assigned by the administration as an official responsibility or undertaken by the teacher voluntarily;

2. "Other official duties," with a heavy accent on committee functions and chaperoning; and

3. Voluntary extracurricular activities with students.

Analysis of these three types of non-academic but inescapable activities discloses that, taken together, they entail an
average of seven hours per week for approximately four-
fifths of the faculty, with the remaining one-fifth falling in a
category either considerably below or considerably above the
average, reflecting a different concentration of duties. Only
one-tenth of the 440 teachers state that they have no official duties beyond their teaching and other direct academic
responsibilities. The official assignments and voluntary activities involved embrace so inclusively the gamut of college life
that it would be a deflection from our purpose to discuss
them here.

In summary, however, we may isolate four facts regarding
non-academic activities. The first is that approximately half
of the teachers' non-academic time devoted to students is occupied with personal counseling. Only two-fifths of the teachers providing clear data are officially assigned to counseling
duty by the administration, but nine-tenths of them engage
in counseling voluntarily.

The second fact is the extent to which the teachers' nonacademic hours are occupied with committees. While a percentage can scarcely be calculated, it is safe from the evidence in the questionnaires to assign at least one-quarter of
the teachers' non-academic but committed hours to this category of work, embracing both official duties and extracurricular activities.

The third fact is that both academic and non-academic
duties differ in accordance with academic responsibility and
status. The full professors represent the most even spread
of activity. The deans are relatively low in teaching load,
but carry a heavier burden of counseling and "other official

duties," than do their colleagues. The heads of departments carry heavy class loads, but their research and counseling correspond fairly closely to that of the teachers as a whole.

The duties of associate professors are generally in line, except that two-thirds spend from twenty-one to forty hours weekly in research, laboratory work, and other auxiliary duties. Assistant professors also carry a heavy load in this field. They are likewise in the upper brackets for teaching, two-thirds reporting fifteen hours or above, while a disproportionate number are in the top bracket of over ten hours for counseling.

Instructors are heavily loaded. Half of them are concentrated in the eleven to fourteen hour teaching group, which is a relatively light schedule, but in addition 50 per cent report between twenty-one and forty hours in research and other auxiliary duties, and two-fifths of them devote from five to ten hours to counseling. The heaviest overall commitment of hours, however, appears to fall on the assistant professors.

Beyond these academic, counseling, and other official duties, the reports show substantial time devoted to voluntary extracurricular activities with students, averaging approximately two hours per week for the two-thirds of the teachers who gave clear information. In addition to general extracurricular activities and to their off-campus church activities, many teachers also devote substantial time to on-campus voluntary religious work with students. Of the three-quarters of the respondees who provide clear information on such religious activity, only 14 per cent report that they give no time to this work, 10 per cent report a fraction of an hour per week, 23 per cent report one hour, 22 per cent two hours, and 14 per cent three hours. Thus 59 per cent of those replying devote from one to three hours weekly to voluntary religious work. An additional 16 per cent contribute substantially more time. We shall await a later stage for evaluation of this activity.

The evidence, in short, bears out the fact that teachers in church-related colleges carry too heavy a load for their own complete satisfaction in their work. In particular, it obliges them to substitute what they often regard as peripheral activity for the stimulating blend of teaching and research which they feel is necessary for professional growth and effectiveness. We shall return to this problem in Chapter 4.

That this frustration does not cause a larger proportion of the teachers to desire to leave their present positions may be due in part to the fact that the overload has been abnormally high since the beginning of World War II in all types of higher educational institutions, and the problem is thus one of degree. As one index to the source of difficulty, the ratio of students to faculty members in a representative group of institutions immediately before the war was eleven to one, whereas in 1946-47 it was fifteen to one. At the same time, the demands for new courses, for increased counseling and for other faculty leadership have been steadily growing.

Growth or Grind?

Facts such as these may seem far removed from the college teacher's religion. They are highly germane, however, to the problem of personal and professional growth on the job, and hence to the religious element as a factor in the teacher's development. For many of the teachers report that so heavy a burden of faculty responsibilities leaves little time and energy for in-service training, personal reflection, and other aspects of rounded self-improvement by the teachers as persons.

In moving from academic and extracurricular responsibilities to current upkeep in professional competence and personal growth, we enter an area where the criteria and the instruments of measurement are not readily at hand. We have attempted to ask some questions which would elicit general information from the teachers on their self-development.

What in-service training, in addition to formal work for academic credit, have the teachers had since they started to teach in college? Practically all of the teachers report some such activity, but it is difficult to assess the value of the varied types of training experience they report. The level of intellectual content, the time and energy involved, the leadership and counsel enlisted, appear to vary greatly from case to case.

Quantitatively, three-fifths of the teachers have participated in informal seminars or conferences related to their subjects; one-third have been in groups on the philosophy and method of teaching; nearly a third have engaged in projects to increase their effectiveness in counseling or other personal work with students; the same number have had an experience of combined teaching and study, either as teaching fellows or otherwise; one-seventh have had their teaching supervised at some time; and one-eighth have participated in projects to increase their effectiveness in religious work with students. An additional 8 per cent report other in-service training activities.

Such "other" activities may be grouped first under co-operative faculty-sponsored projects, including the following: "faculty workshops," "faculty reading circles," "faculty studies," "faculty self-surveys," "special campus committees." Many stress, of course, regular faculty and departmental meetings as having special value, while others decry these meetings.

There is a reasonable complement of references to "articles read on my own" and to special summer school courses. One teacher mentions specifically "summer workshops in higher education." Others have profited from courses in audio-visual aids, teaching methods, or testing methods. There are a number of references to interinstitutional activities such as "conferences on education," "convention work," "state, regional and national meetings," "North Central Association Workshop."

In the realm of practical work in one's academic field, we get from sociologists "community work with Negroes in the South," activities in "local social agencies," "research and travel on subjects of resettlement, colonization, co-operatives." One English teacher finds help in "dramatics," another in serving as a "research assistant" and another in doing "journalism for the state press." A teacher of economics and commercial subjects cites "practical accounting" as an aid in his professional growth.

A number of teachers cite activities of a religious character. One mentions "the Lutheran faculty conference meeting." Another states, "I consider my occasional pulpit work as very helpful." A sociology teacher is helped by working as a "student summer service worker under the Board of Home Missions in the Congregational Church." A woman teacher mentions "Y.W.C.A., Wesley House, Girls' Circle." One teacher refers by name to a former senior colleague in another college who "gave me great help—informally and by example."

Finally, there are a number of good words for "professional society meetings and periodicals," "professional evaluation projects," "counseling meetings," "A.A.U.P. meetings."

Of the persons whom these statements represent, over half have doctoral degrees or are to receive their doctorates within a very short time. Over half of the remainder have had graduate courses in education. The fact that this high a proportion of the group volunteering their own ideas have had this much training may suggest a greater awareness of the issues on the part of those with such background.

To what extent do the teachers participate in professional societies and similar associations? Over four-fifths indicate one or more such groups of which they are members. One-fourth report membership in the American Association of University Professors, one-eighth in Phi Beta Kappa, and one-sixteenth in the American Association of University Women. The A.A.U.W. members comprise one-fourth of the women in the study. Membership in one or more other national societies claims three-fourths of the teachers, and in one or more regional societies claims one-third. Six teachers are in international societies. Many of our respondents hold offices and carry responsibilities which exceed simple membership. There is little indication, however, as to how meaningful the reported leadership may be.

Some incidental disclosures are of interest. One dean states that he is on the national Board of Higher Education of the Disciples of Christ. A full professor with a Ph. D., after presenting a list of societies, concludes "but at present have failed to renew membership for financial reasons." Still another Ph. D. professor reports that he is a member of twenty-one professional societies. At the opposite pole, the following is too choice to omit: "None; they are ridiculous and boring groups of scholars who can't teach—politicians!"

Closely related to professional societies and responsibilities are the answers regarding special leadership assumed by the teachers beyond their own institutions in their respective fields of study, such as speaking, writing, guest lectureships, recognitions, and awards. It is difficult to measure the results of this inquiry. Though there are some notable exceptions, the net impression is not one of great vigor, vision, or initiative. Unquestionably a reason for this, referred to by many as a difficulty, is the overload of work which we already have mentioned. Thus one professor, again a Ph. D., attempts to speak for his colleagues: "*Nobody* on our faculty does much of this—no materials for research readily available, no money or leisure, no sabbaticals, heavy teaching schedules, pitifully low salaries."

This is an unhappy commentary on a field of intellectual and spiritual endeavor with such limitless potentialities as the church-related college. It leads to an examination of another area of data—the reading habits of the teachers in their personal, non-professional lives.

To make our question specific, we asked for "some of the books on cultural or religious subjects outside your field which you have read in the last year." The 220 teachers supplying information had read an average of 2.8 such books apiece during the preceding year, representing 323 separate titles. The wide variety of reading is suggested by the fact that 242 of the books were listed by only one person each, leaving only eighty-one which were mentioned twice or more. Of these only eighteen were read by 3 per cent or more of the responding teachers. The titles and percentages of these leading books are indicated in the following table:

TABLE IV

Books Read by the Largest Number of Teachers
(Based on 220 replies)

	% of Teachers
Toynbee, Arnold J., *A Study of History*, 1947	15
Du Nuoy, Pierre Lecomte, *Human Destiny*, 1947	13
Liebman, Joshua L., *Peace of Mind*, 1946	10
Lewis, C. S., the works of, contemporary	9
Trueblood, Elton D., the works of, contemporary	7
The Bible	6
Douglas, Lloyd C., the works of, contemporary	6
Fosdick, Harry Emerson, the works of, contemporary	4
Jones, E. Stanley, the works of, contemporary	4
Schweitzer, Albert, the works of, contemporary	4
Fisher, Jonathan, the works of, early 18th century	4
Niebuhr, Reinhold, the works of, contemporary	4
Peale, Norman V., *Guide to Confident Living*, 1948	3
Barzun, Jacques, *Teacher in America*, 1945	3
Plato, the works of, 4th century B.C.	3
Poetry, miscellaneous	3
Sorokin, Pitirim A., *The Crisis of Our Age*, 1941	3
Whitehead, Alfred N., the works of, contemporary	3

Analysis of the total reading reveals an average of a book a year by each respondee in the field of religion. While the primary religious concern of the questionnaire may have elicited books of this category in larger proportion than other books which the teacher did not mention, the result is nevertheless an evidence of religious interest on the part of the teachers. Moreover, a comparison of the 220 teachers who replied with the equal number who did not reply or who replied inconclusively, reveals no generally atypical characteristics on the part of the ones who gave information, thus tending to confirm the representativeness of the result.

It is not surprising that the Bible, though near the top with thirteen listings, is not mentioned more frequently. Evidence elsewhere in the questionnaires indicates that this does not reflect the extent to which the Bible is read. Thus at least half of the listings of different church responsibilities involve activities in which the use of the Bible would appear to be inescapable. Very likely many readers of the Bible failed to mention it because they assumed that the Bible was to be taken for granted. Or again, it is improbable that the entire Bible was read during this one year by many, if any, of the teachers, and they may have regarded it on this ground as disqualified. These possible explanations are based only on inference. There is no clear evidence in this study as to how widely or profoundly the Bible is studied.

The information concerning other religious reading is more conclusive. One notable fact is the great spread of material. Among the eighteen leading authors for all types of reading, the nine in the order of frequency whose cited works may clearly be classed as religious are C. S. Lewis, Elton D. Trueblood, Lloyd C. Douglas, Harry Emerson Fosdick, E. Stanley Jones, Albert Schweitzer, Jonathan Fisher, Reinhold Niebuhr, and Norman Vincent Peale. Taking successive couplings among other religious books mentioned more than once, the wide variety is even more striking. We note Norman Vincent Peale followed shortly by Augustine; Thomas Aquinas matched with books on Bible prophecy; Emil Brunner with Henry J. Cadbury; T. S. Eliot with Nels F. S. Ferré; Hazen Foundation pamphlets with Thomas S.

Kepler; Frank C. Laubach with Henry C. Link; miscellaneous Church School study books with Donald M. Baillie; Karl Barth with George A. Barton; Søren A. Kierkegaard with Kenneth Scott Latourette; A. J. Muste with Fulton Oursler; J. B. Phillips with George Santayana; Jean Paul Sartre with Dorothy L. Sayers; and R. H. Tawney with Chad Walsh! Whatever else may be said of college teachers' religious reading, no single author or sectarian viewpoint is sweeping the field.

A second commentary is the predominance of very recent or at least generally contemporary religious writings. This may be explained in part by the confinement of the question to the last year, but if this year is typical, most of the classical religious reading, if any, was done before the teachers started teaching. Indeed, the great bulk of the reading in all areas is from fairly recent works. There is neither censure nor approbation in this observation. It simply is one angle in our teacher profile.

The further fact is manifest, and entirely understandable, that most of the religious reading is not technical or highly specialized. Books with a strong strain of personal helpfulness and semipopular interpretation predominate.

Pursuing our companion interest in religion and in education, the latter area is less well represented in the reports. The qualifying phrase "outside your field" may have been interpreted by many of the teachers to exclude books in the total field of education. This is a possible explanation for the paucity of reading reported, for example, on the profound current problems confronting higher education today. The gap here is worthy of a more extensive analysis than this study can undertake. Any negative impression from this list may be somewhat mitigated, however, when we discuss later the writings of other teachers which our present teachers have found helpful at some time in their careers.

There is relatively extensive reading in current socio-economic-historical, psychological-philosophical and other serious non-fiction areas. These readings correspond broadly to the ratings in the popular best-selling lists of the two years preceding the inquiry, suggesting that the reading of college teachers in those fields is much the same as that of the general public. As a corollary, the reading of classical and semi-classical authors, whether in the field of fact or fiction, is relatively meager.

What we have observed about both subject matter and period is made readily visible in the following summaries:

TABLE V

TEACHER READING DIVIDED ACCORDING TO SUBJECTS AND PERIODS
(Based on 220 Teachers' Replies)

Subjects	% of Total Listings
Religion (diverse)	35
Current socio-economic-historical	17
Current psychology and philosophy	14
Current miscellaneous non-fiction	6
Education (diverse)	6
Current fiction	5
Current cultural (art, music, etc.)	4
Classical non-fiction (Greek predominantly)	4
Current biography	3
Miscellaneous poetry, drama, and fiction	2
Current poetry, drama, and literary criticism	2
Classical fiction, drama, poetry	1
Current science	1
Non-current miscellaneous non-fiction	—
Totals	100%
Periods	
1945-1949 (current)	43
1900-1944 (broadly contemporary)	46
19th century	2
Pre-19th century (to early Christian)	3
Early Christian	3
Antiquity	3
Totals	100%

Turning briefly to magazines, we find that the two-thirds of the teachers giving definite information read an average of

3.2 publications regularly. Many of the comments we have made concerning the books they read apply equally to magazines. Religion is well represented, though not as strongly as in the case of books. *The Christian Century*, with eighty-five listings, is outstandingly high, ranking second only to the *Atlantic Monthly*. No other religious publication is cited more than six times, but below this number there are frequent listings of separate religious magazines. There is a fair aggregate balance between denominational and ecumenical publications, but a less creditable balance in the cases of many individual respondents.

Publications which might generally be classed as current socio-economic-historical again stand high, as with the books. Education publications and literary magazines are relatively low. No journal devoted to religion in higher education is cited. There is quite naturally a greater concentration upon a few outstandingly popular choices, as the variety of commendable magazines is less great than is the case with books. The leading selections, like the book choices, correspond in general to the circulation of the magazines among the general public. In the field of journals emanating from educational institutions, the *Yale Review* is the only magazine associated with a particular university which is mentioned by more than one teacher. The high ranking of this publication is especially notable in view of the fact, as we have seen, that Yale stands as low as eighteenth in the number of the teachers who have studied there.

We shall have occasion later to mention the reading of the teachers in relation to their training, particularly in areas directly germane to their philosophy as teachers. To make the foregoing paragraphs more specific, we list in Table VI the magazines which were mentioned by 3 per cent or more of the responding teachers.

This completes our faculty profile. We have thought it useful to picture these teachers, in broad strokes, before exam-

TABLE VI

MAGAZINES READ BY THE LARGEST NUMBER OF TEACHERS
(Based on 305 replies)

	% of Teachers
Atlantic Monthly	31
Christian Century	28
Harper's Magazine	25
Time	16
Reader's Digest	13
Saturday Review of Literature	13
Life	8
New Yorker	7
The Nation	7
National Geographic	6
American Scholar	5
New Republic	5
New York Times Magazine	4
Fortune	4
News Week	4
Yale Review	4
Fellowship	3
Saturday Evening Post	3

ining their religious beliefs. We have sought to portray their early impulse and motivation to teach, their academic training, their teaching experience and present responsibilities, and the character of their efforts to grow as teachers and as persons. We shall now attempt to report and analyze the beliefs and practices of the teachers in the areas of central concern to this study.

3.

FACULTY RELIGION: THE TEACHER'S BELIEFS AND PRACTICES IN THEIR BEARING UPON HIS LIFE WORK

WE RETURN to our opening question: What are the religious beliefs and practices of the teachers in relation to the mission of the church-related college, and how do the teachers conceive their role as a part of that mission?

We have noted that many of the teachers consider college teaching as a strategic Christian vocation. For half of them this conception was a factor in the selection of their life work. In this chapter we shall examine the fruits of that view in the present personal faith of the teachers and in their philosophy and practice of religion in relation to higher education. We shall begin with the traditional avenue of Christian expression, participation in the life of the Church.

Church Affiliation and Activity

It is common knowledge, and entirely to be expected, that the faculty members of church-related institutions should be members of churches and should assume leadership commensurate with their ability, training, and standing in the community. Thus 95 per cent of the teachers report their church affiliation, while only 4 per cent indicate that they are not members and 1 per cent fail to answer. Nor is it surprising in Protestant colleges and universities that some of their teachers should be non-Protestant. The presence among the

43

440 teachers of one Roman Catholic, one Jew, and seventeen persons of no affiliation is consonant with the freedom of Protestantism.

The denominational affiliations of the teachers correspond in 56 per cent of the cases to the affiliations of the respective institutions in which they serve. The total number of teachers of the respective confessional groups also is approximately equal in most cases to the total number of teachers reporting from the colleges related to those groups.

Very few institutions confine their faculty rigidly to members of their own denominations, but there is a variance in practice in this regard from one denomination—and even one institution—to another. Some denominations appear to draw heavily upon other groups for their teachers, while some recruit a larger proportion from their own ranks. The denominations whose figures are sufficiently large to supply a dependable index reveal some interesting differences. These are indicated in the following table:

TABLE VII

ANALYSIS OF THE COLLEGES OF THE LARGER DENOMINATIONS IN RELATION
TO THE CHURCH AFFILIATIONS OF THEIR TEACHERS

	Teachers from Same Denomination Per cent	Teachers from Other Denominations Per cent
Lutheran (all branches)	73	27
Baptist, Southern	72	28
Disciples	67	33
Presbyterian U. S.	58	42
Methodist	56	44
Congregational Christian	55	45
Protestant Episcopal	53	47
Baptist, Northern	52	48
Presbyterian U. S. A.	41	59

Statistically, these groups differ significantly from one another.[5] Moreover, the Lutheran and Presbyterian U.S.A. col-

---

[5] $X^2 = 18.67$; $P = .03$.

leges differ significantly from the average for all groups.[6] The Lutheran colleges appear to draw their teachers largely from their own denominations, while the Presbyterian U.S.A. colleges represent the opposite trend. The other denominations in the list do not show important variations.

Several denominations appear to be better represented generally among teachers in the church-related colleges than are others. In most cases the figures for the respective groups are too small to justify generalizations from the data. In the cases of larger groups, on the other hand, interest may attach to one significant deviation. The Episcopalians are disproportionately represented among the teachers as a whole, there being twice as many Episcopalians as the total number of teachers from Episcopal institutions. They are spread among twenty-three colleges and universities, representing eleven denominations. The Congregational Christians and Presbyterians U.S.A. also show an oversupply of teachers, but the discrepancy is not significant.

Given these facts concerning church affiliation, what is the evidence regarding church participation? Here we shall not examine denominational variations. The majority of the teachers, embracing 52 per cent, attend church services from thirty-one to fifty-two times a year, while 15 per cent attend from eleven to thirty times, 10 per cent from none to ten times, and the remaining 18 per cent who give a clear reply attend from fifty-three to more than 104 times a year.

The amount of time devoted to other activities in the work of the church is less consistent. Twenty-six per cent of the teachers report a zero, in addition to 17 per cent who fail to answer, or who indicate uncertainty. It is of interest that 43 per cent spend an average of two hours per week in church work, and that 11 per cent spend from four to ten hours.

---

[6] Lutheran: $CR = +1.96$; $P = .05$; Presbyterian, U.S.A., $CR = -2.57$; $P = .01$.

On the whole, therefore, the time and energy devoted to leadership in the church, embracing at least twenty types of activity, indicates that the teachers in church-related colleges assume a large share of responsibility in the congregations of which they are members. It is not clear to what extent their church leadership relates them closely to their students. Only 1 per cent specify programs for students among their church responsibilities. Other activities in their churches doubtless bring them together with students, but there is no evidence that this is a predominant area of the teachers' concern in their church life. Any lack of carry-over which there may be in this regard finds a more significant and tangible counterpart in data we shall examine presently concerning the frequent gap between religious conviction and communication of that conviction to students.

Belief and Its Nurture

Ninety-four per cent of the teachers, including seventy per cent of those who indicate no church affiliation, regard themselves as Christians, "interpreting the meaning of Christian in their own terms," while only 2 per cent do not so regard themselves. The remainder are uncertain or do not answer. These and later data indicate that many teachers do not consider church membership as necessary to being a Christian. There are many correlations and many striking absences of correlation between particular church affiliations and answers to numerous questions. These will be examined in due course.

It is not surprising that the teachers who consider themselves to be Christians have widely varying views of God. The small number of nine teachers who definitely do not regard themselves as Christians comprise two atheists, one humanist-idealist, one deist, one whom we can not classify, and —interestingly enough—four who check the most orthodox view of God. It is possible that some answered negatively because, though they are Christians in concept, they do not feel that they are worthy of being called Christians in all the implications of the term.

Because of the importance of the teachers' replies on their views of God, and the bearing of this question on later questions, we present in Table VIII a summary of the answers on this central tenet of belief. The proffered definitions are listed in the order of frequency checked, rather than in the order in which they appeared in the questionnaire. The latter order is indicated in Appendix I.

TABLE VIII

THE TEACHERS' CONCEPTIONS OF GOD

	No. of Teachers	% of Teachers
1. God is the Father of our Lord Jesus Christ, and of all mankind; Maker of heaven and earth, unto whom all hearts are open, all desires known, and from whom no secrets are hid; whom to know is perfect peace	216	49
2. God is a sovereign, righteous Being, Creator of the universe and of natural laws, who through his laws rules the universe. In a special sense man is his creature, and Jesus is the supreme example of how man may know and serve God aright. The protection and favor of God can be supplicated through worship and prayer	96	22
3. God is the Power making for the increase of meaning and value	42	10
4. God is the omnipotent Creator of the universe and of natural laws, and rules the universe through these laws. It is possible that he may be accessible to man and may be subject to man's supplications	28	6
5. God is a projection of human ideals and desires	18	4
6. God is Absolute Mind	8	2
7. God is another name for natural law	6	1
8. I do not believe in God at all	3	1
9. Other more adequate view (specified)	15	3
10. Uncertain or unspecified	8	2
	440	100%

Seventy-one per cent of the teachers checked the first two formulations. This heavy concentration reflects a general conformity to the prevailing Christian concepts of divinity. While both are clearly within the Christian tradition, the first group may be considered the more "orthodox" because of its pronounced Christocentric position, couched broadly in the terms of the Apostles' Creed. The second definition probably was selected by the more "liberal," but still traditional, Christians. With a less exacting Christology, it corresponds broadly to the Pelagian position.

The definition of God as the Power making for the increase of meaning and value may be variously catalogued, but the comments of a number of the respondents checking this option would suggest that they are theistic naturalists. One of them mentions Henry Nelson Wieman by name. The fourth position, describing God as omnipotent Creator, with elaborations, may be broadly termed as deistic. There may be room for argument as to whether this should be regarded as within the Christian tradition.

We observe the small number who take the psychological projection view, and the small number of absolute idealists, out-and-out naturalists, and atheists. The 3 per cent whom we have classed as "other" embrace those who made comments but whose statements can not be classified. Prevailingly they adopt various rationalist positions which would not qualify within any of the definitions provided, but which we may broadly term "philosophical." The 2 per cent whom we call "uncertain or unspecified" include those who indicate that they do not know what their views are, or who prefer not to state them.

It should be stated that 11 per cent within the first category, 1 per cent in the second category, and 1 per cent in the third category represent persons who did not simply check the indicated captions but either combined two or more captions or furnished new or modified definitions. That this was done in so many cases results from the fact that many of the stated formulations are not mutually exclusive. The largest number of mergers were within the first and second positions, in which cases the first answer has been counted, as it represents the more specific and hence the more distinguishing of the two positions, while fully embracing the second one. The majority of the teachers making their own comments propose further precision, not subtraction or emasculation, of the various definitions offered.

Adopting a broad classification, consistent with the teachers' own conception of themselves as Christians, we may consider at least the first four categories, totalling 87 per cent, as within the orbit of Christian theism. It is interesting that this is somewhat less than the 94 per cent who, as we have seen, regard themselves as Christians. We found elsewhere in the study that not only the group representing this discrepancy, but the great majority of the teachers, consider other criteria as more important than theistic or related intellectual concepts in determining whether a man is a Christian. Thus, 73 per cent of them largely agree, and only 10 per cent definitely disagree, with the statement of J. H. Oldham that "what makes a man a Christian is neither his intellectual acceptance of certain ideas nor his conformity to a certain rule, but his possession of a certain spirit and his participation in a certain life."[7]

Also, it is apparent that lack of church affiliation does not mean atheism. Among the 5 per cent who are not members of churches, only two teachers do not believe in God. On the other side, one of the three professed atheists is a member of a church, while another, who neither believes in God nor belongs to a church regards himself as a Christian.

The views of God correspond in a striking degree to denominational affiliations. Noting from the answers certain broad trends according to church groupings, we found the

---

[7] J. H. Oldham, from a quotation in the *Methodist Student Bulletin*, January, 1949, p. 8.

Southern Baptists, the various Lutheran groups, the Presbyterians U. S., the Reformed, and the smaller evangelical denominations to be prevailingly conservative in their theism, while the Congregational Christians, Methodists, Episcopalians, Negro groups, and teachers of no affiliation were prevailingly liberal. In between were the Northern Baptists, Disciples, Friends, and Presbyterians U. S. A.[8]

The study reveals great variation in the extent to which theistic concepts have a bearing on other concepts and practices. We may illustrate this discrepancy by noting the teachers' views on some important religious beliefs, and then comparing them with their views of God. Table IX presents the distribution of answers by all 440 teachers to a number of indicative questions.

We note the wide spread of these questions. They embrace the character of scriptural authority, the conception of the distinctive Christian community, the importance of communion with the divine, the understanding of the nature of man as a creature of God, the issue of man's goodness or depravity, and the problem of salvation. Taken together with the view of God, we have in these data a good general index to the teachers' religious beliefs. With two exceptions which we shall presently note, these replies confirm the impression of broad conformity to tradition in the area of concepts.

Analysis of the answers of individual teachers discloses a close correlation between view of God and other strictly religious concepts. The proportion of negative replies corresponds to the degree of non-conformity in the view of God. Thus the persons who check the most Christocentric view of God average only 4 per cent in their negative answers to the questions above except 10a and 13a and those with the Pelagian view show 5 per cent for the same questions, while

---

[8] On a Chi-square test of these combinations, the deviations in their views of God proved to be highly significant. $X^2 = 53.22$; $P = .0001$.

TABLE IX

THE TEACHERS' VIEWS ON CERTAIN RELIGIOUS QUESTIONS
(The identifying numerical captions refer to the
Questionnaire, Part B)

	% Yes	% No	% Uncertain, Qualified, or No Answer
9a. Do you consider the Bible to be religiously authoritative?	69	14	17
10a. Do you regard church membership to be a necessary part of the Christian life?	54	36	10
11a. Do you regard prayer as necessary to the Christian life?	77	13	10
12a. Do you derive your concept, whatever it may be, of the worthfulness of human life and the brotherhood of man from your view of God?	75	10	15
13a. Do you agree largely with the following statement: "Man is fundamentally good and his inherent goodness is indicated in his increasing capacity, by using his intelligence, to solve the problems that confront him"?[9]	42	35	23
13e. Do you believe that all men stand in need of divine salvation through Christ, in whatever way you understand this concept?	72	14	14

the theistic naturalists show 32 per cent, and those in the "philosophical" categories average 44 per cent.

The two exceptions to which we have referred concern questions 10a on church membership and 13a on the nature of man. We remove them from the above analysis of negative answers because on these two questions the disagreement is so great as to constitute an almost nullifying divergence. The ministers of the churches to which the teachers belong probably represent the same diversity of opinion.

However, the views concerning church membership in 10a again correspond broadly to the views of God. In view of the

---

[9] Nash, Arnold S., *The University and the Modern World*, New York: The Macmillan Company, 1944, p. 30.

wide split on this question between yes and no answers, we examined them all, and found highly significant correlations. The theistic naturalists and the teachers holding the "philosophical" views of God deviate to an important degree toward negative answers on the necessity of church membership, the teachers of the deistic and Pelagian views conform closely to the average for all teachers, and the teachers of the Christocentric view deviate significantly toward positive answers.[10]

Question 13a regarding the goodness of man calls for special analysis. The quotation cited is taken from Arnold S. Nash's critique of what he characterizes as the prevailing "liberalism" of contemporary university thought. He considers this mental outlook to be in part a child of the purely scientific approach to truth, glorifying the powers of the intellect, and in part a Christian heresy, denying the true character of man as both good and evil.

We desired to discover whether this appraisal is valid for faculty members in church-related colleges. The fact that most of the teachers are fairly evenly divided on this question, and that 23 per cent are too uncertain to return a definite answer, is a clear intimation that the group we are studying includes a substantial proportion who depart from the pattern Nash has described. This is not a commentary on Nash's appraisal of the mental outlook, or "dogma," as he calls it, of the university world as a whole, as we do not possess the evidence to make an evaluation of all teachers in higher education. But in any measure that he is correct, the faculties of church-related colleges would appear to present a departure from the norm of unrelieved optimism on the nature of man.

Not only do a large proportion of the teachers disavow the

---

[10] These divergences are reflected in the following critical ratios: theistic naturalists, $CR = -4.79$; $P = .000001$; "philosophical" group, $CR = -4.59$; $P = .000002$; Christocentric group, $CR = +4.05$; $P = .00003$.

"liberal" definition of man, but 183 of them, representing 83 per cent of the respondents who do not accept the view, provide their own modifications of or substitutions for the proffered statement. These comments, as is the case with the view of God, would constitute sufficient material for a separate chapter if this were our major concern in the study.

Suffice it here to say that of the 183 teachers making comments, 25 per cent believe that man is essentially evil, and 38 per cent believe that he has the capacity for both good and evil. Some of the latter stress personal free will, others the grace of God, and still others the conditioning influence of external environment, as the determinants of man's individual character. Those who believe that man is fundamentally depraved usually emphasize salvation through Christ, often in highly technical language. One affirms, "Man is born in sin and needs to be born again by believing in the shed blood of the Lord Jesus to atone for his sins." Others, without going into detail, simply state that they are Calvinists. One teacher feels he has made his own position clear when he asserts, "The above statement is contrary to Lutheran theology."

On the other hand, approximately an equal number refer to the need of faith in God in addition to the need of intelligence, but do not delimit their concepts doctrinally. These usually are the teachers who believe man has the capacity for both good and evil; those with this belief are invariably the ones who have faith in conditioning. A small number of teachers holding various views on the nature of man are convinced that his primary need in addition to intelligence is greater love for his fellow-men.

None of the teachers repudiate intelligence, but all of them who mention it feel that it alone is inadequate. Beyond the strictly theological issue, 12 per cent of the teachers point out that if man is solving his problems by intelligence, he is doing a very poor job of it.

Three teachers reject the terms "good" and "evil" entirely. A sociologist states, "The dualism of good and evil appears to me as a meaningless dichotomy that interferes with scientific investigation of human relationships." A teacher of physics feel that "such moral judgments are primarily extensions of childish judgments as to what is found pleasing or satisfying of the childish desires."

Four teachers prefer not to think of man, but to consider individual men, some of whom they consider fundamentally good and some fundamentally bad. There appear, in short, to be as many views in these matters in the colleges as there are in our society at large.

The patterns of teacher response on this issue show no significant correlation between doctrine of man (if so formal a term may be applied) and view of God. Thus, of the 216 teachers with the most orthodox theistic view, 41 per cent agree with the statement, while 40 per cent disagree. The Pelagians show 46 per cent agreeing and 33 per cent disagreeing. The deists are 39 per cent for, 25 per cent against, while the theistic naturalists divide 36 per cent and 33 per cent. The three atheists are split at two for and one against, while the teachers in other categories divide 43 per cent for and 31 per cent against. Part of the reason for the wide diversity of view and for an apparent lack of correspondence between view of man and view of God is undoubtedly that so many other factors than theistic concepts enter into this question. This tends to suggest what will be further documented later—that the farther one gets from areas which the teachers consider to be religious, the less are they influenced by their particular view of God.

Beyond concepts, what do we find concerning the personal religious nurture and self-expression of these teachers? How do they grow religiously and to what extent do they share their religious life with one another? By far the largest number cite two avenues of religious growth, 64 per cent by "seeking to apply their religious conviction to concrete problems" and 60 per cent by "engaging in public worship including hearing sermons."

Apart from these two disciplines, no other means of nurture is cited by as many as half the teachers. Forty-seven per cent derive help from "pondering their own subject-matter field in its religious bearings," 45 per cent from reading the Bible, 43 per cent by engaging in personal devotions, and 38 per cent by reading books of inspiration on religious subjects. Approximately one-fourth of the teachers derive help from studying the truths of other religions and from studying the intellectual formulations of the Christian faith, showing 26 per cent each. Far down the line we find 16 per cent who find aid in family devotions, and 10 per cent who are helped by courses or informal group studies in religion.

A number of teachers name other aids to their religious growth, but these do not add materially to our information. The impression which is left by most of the 86 per cent of the teachers who answer this question is one of genuine spiritual earnestness. There is evidence that the teachers are honestly reporting actuality in their religious life rather than mere desire. As an example, only 10 per cent indicate that they are now finding help through informal group studies in religion, but 50 per cent "feel the need of intimate, informal discussions and fellowship with other faculty members around common religious interests," and only 37 per cent state definitely that they do not feel such a need.

Groups for the purpose of such discussion and fellowship exist on campuses represented by 17 per cent of the teachers, and 71 per cent of these teachers participate in the groups. Of the teachers on campuses where such a group does not exist or where the teacher is uncertain about its existence, 51 per cent state that they would participate if there were such a group, while 16 per cent would not, and 26 per cent are understandably uncertain.

The net conclusion from this information is that roughly one-half of the faculty members consulted feel the need for help toward religious self-expression and personal growth in community with faculty colleagues, but that only about a sixth have such an opportunity through existing groups on their campuses and that only a tenth appear to be aware of such opportunities. This clearly is an area of significant need among the teachers in the church-related colleges.

To what extent do the expressions of need for such religious community correspond to particular religious leanings as reflected in the teachers' views of God? Here, where we have moved from the area of concept to that of personal religious expression, there is a less clear progression, if any, from the persons of one theistic view to those of another. Thus 57 per cent of the Christocentric group desire such a faculty group activity, 50 per cent of the Pelagians, 61 per cent of the deists, 45 per cent of the theistic naturalists, and 22 per cent of the "others." The atheists include one who desires such activity. Apart from the "others," who are characteristically low, the figures for the principal categories are thus confusingly close together.

It appears, in short, that there is a broad but significant consistency between the view of God and views on other conceptual religious questions, but that on issues of religious practice the results are unclear. We shall examine as occasion arises the relation of the concept of God to beliefs and practices in areas not exclusively religious. First we turn to the views of our teachers on issues in which religion has a bearing upon educational philosophy.

Religion and Education

One of our objects in this study is to determine what relation there may be between religious concepts and educational concepts. It will be helpful at the outset to present in table form the answers of all the teachers to a series of questions in which both of these spheres of thought are involved. Though apologies are in order for the length of the list, it represents a gleaning and reorganization of far more voluminous data. The material is presented in one table to place it in a common perspective, affording comparability.

TABLE X

THE TEACHERS' PHILOSOPHY OF RELIGION AND EDUCATION
(The identifying numerical captions refer to the
Questionnaire, Part B)

	% Yes	% No	% Uncertain, Qualified, or No Answer
1a. Do you agree in general that "true education is not an end in itself but a means to an end: service to one's day and generation"?[11]	89	3	8
3a. Are there irreconcilable conflicts between the Christian religion and some of the findings of science or history?....	8	84	8
5a. Do you agree in general that "there is but one sure road of access to truth —the road of patient, cooperative inquiry, operating by means of observation, experiment, record, and controlled reflections?"[12]	65	24	11
5c. Do you interpret the realm of value in your subject matter field?	89	2	9
14a. Do you believe that your religious faith places limitations upon your objective search for and communication of truth?	5	90	5
15a. Do you consider divine revelation, as you understand it, to be compatible			

---

[11] Quotation from address delivered by President Kenneth I. Brown of Denison University to the faculty of Queens College, Charlotte, North Carolina, at their annual faculty in-service training conference in 1948. Taken from the report of the Conference, *Education for Christian Citizenship*, p. 9. This and the other questions in Table VIII have been abbreviated to save space. The full formulations appear in the Questionnaire.

[12] John Dewey, *A Common Faith*, New Haven: Yale University Press, 1936, pp. 31-32.

	% Yes	% No	% Uncertain, Qualified, or No Answer
with human reason as a valid means of access to truth?	70	10	20
15b. Does your religious conviction and experience give you added insights in your subject matter field?	71	16	13
16b. Is God, as you understand Him, the central reality lending unity to truth?	77	6	17
17d. Do you agree in general that "what makes a man a Christian is neither his intellectual acceptance of certain ideas nor his conformity to a certain rule, but his possession of a certain spirit and his participation in a certain life"?[13]	73	10	17
18. Do you believe that the college professor who seeks to relate his Christian view to his teaching is in danger of:			
a. Sectarianism	18	50	32
b. Dogmatism	19	47	34
c. Obscurantism	12	46	42
d. Substitution of piety for sound scholarship	18	44	38

The fact which stands out in these and other replies is that the great majority of the teachers appear to have satisfied their own minds that any conflict between the methods of education and the methods of religion is not only resolvable but largely resolved. While the size of the majority varies, the aggregate result is fairly conclusive.

The first question does not explicitly involve religion, but the clear disavowal of education as an end in itself suggests a world view in which other and more ultimate norms have higher claim. Such a *Weltanschauung* makes room for the place of religious loyalties, which in the case of our teachers become specific at other points in our study.

The next question, and others which could be cited, put

---

[13] Oldham, *loc cit.*

our teachers clearly on record as reconciling science and religion. There are no important differences according to teaching fields, but there is a striking deviation according to views of God. The proponents of the varied "philosophical" positions return a ratio of negative responses on the compatibility of science and religion which shows a significant statistical deviation from the norm for all the teachers.[14]

This result appears to suggest that some of the philosophers are chary of what they consider the Christian world view to be, and are more reluctant to grant a reconciliation between science and religion as they understand it than are the teachers whose views of God are more conventional. This accords with evidence elsewhere in the study that some of the teachers, regarding themselves as "emancipated," hold an unenlightened view as to what the Christian religion in its intellectual framework represents. But the primary point now is that apart from this minority group, most of the teachers believe that they have achieved a reconciliation between science and religion.

There are three sets of contrasts, however, in the foregoing table. In the first place, there is an evident inconsistency between the common hospitality accorded by most of the teachers to both divine revelation and human reason in 15a, and the serious difficulty some of the teachers confessed with the formulation of 5a. These questions were purposely spaced in the questionnaire so that their juxtaposition would not be obvious. The results suggest confusion in the minds of the teachers, though we must make allowance for possible failure to comprehend the questions, especially 5a. Here, before we had injected the concept of revelation, we found 65 per cent of the teachers accepting without question a statement which they may not have recognized as made by John Dewey. The authorship is not important to our present ob-

---

[14] CR = 3.24; P = .001.

servation. The significant fact is that within the categories of the teachers' customary approach to the problem of truth, two-thirds of them were largely satisfied with this "scientific" description of how to attain truth. In 15a, on the other hand, where they were consciously confronting a question of religion, 70 per cent of the teachers considered divine revelation to be compatible with human reason as a means of access to truth, and only 10 per cent did not consider it compatible.

This reveals a problem of dichotomy between the teacher's belief conceptually in revealed truth and his practice educationally as if the sole avenues to truth were through the processes of the human mind. Between his personal religious life and his professional life—as is the case with men of most vocations—he seems to have difficulty in finding a common universe of discourse. We must not labor this point, nor would it be worthy of note except that evidence which we find later points to the same separation. Our present illustration is in the realm of concept, and may be too theoretical to be serious. Later data reveal the existence of the problem at the work-a-day level.

Lest we leave the impression that the teachers were oblivious to this difficulty, the fact that nearly a third as many answered 5a negatively as answered it positively indicates arrested attention and the unreadiness of many teachers to accept the "scientific" method as sufficient. Moreover, it is notable that of the 138 teachers who indicated disagreement with or uncertainty concerning the formulation, four-fifths offered their own modifications. Of this group, the great majority called attention in one form or another to the problem we are discussing.

The list of alternative avenues to truth which our teachers offer would do credit to a glossary on mysticism. Thus "revelation" is mentioned by twenty-nine teachers, "intuition" by twenty-three, "insight" by eight, "mysticism" by seven, "God" by seven, "faith" by six, "religious faith" by six, "sudden or accidental" truth by five, "the Bible" by four, "inspiration" by four. To these are added from one to three times each such words as "prayer," "illumination," "vision," "spiritual perception," "the guidance of the Holy Spirit," "religious experience," "imagination," "judgment," "the emotional," "feeling," "deduction," "Gestalt learning," "the supernatural," "moral values," "apprehension," "the inner light," "philosophy," "poetry," "higher reasoning," "aesthetic truth." One teacher asserts "God is truth," another "Christ is truth."

The most precise theological formula for arriving at truth comes from a teacher who embraces several conditions in the fewest possible words: "revelation in answer to prayer by the Holy Spirit." Most of the respondents, however, are less doctrinal in their comments. Answers such as the following are more frequent: "I believe that a person can not dig up spiritual truths by the above methods. They are too complex and, I believe, must be accepted without proof." Or again, the suggested formula is "only part of the road. Overestimating the importance of the rational factor is a common academic error." Equally to the point: "This road is vitally important (but) to say 'there is but one' is narrow thinking."

Neither of the last two comments refers necessarily to the religious apprehension of truth. Many of the teachers, particularly in English, are equally concerned at the limitations of the statement from the point of view of spiritual values not primarily associated with religion. One sociologist says, "I regard poetry as capable of presenting truth. I don't think imagination is limited to scientific method." In similar vein, "I believe in the efficiency of the scientific method in realms of natural and social science; but other methods of 'revelation' are also valid, in fields of art and religious expression." Again, "I would try to make some distinction between scientific, social, historical, etc., truth and spiritual, mystical truth which the sciences—natural, social and psychological—have not taught us to tabulate."

Other teachers question the formula not on religious or aesthetic grounds but philosophically. One accepts the statement if it is confined to "the realm of the empirical," while another states, "If one holds to the Positivism of Comte, the 'road of patient, co-operative inquiry,' etc. will not result in apprehending ultimate truths. One must respect the judgment of the higher intuitions. One's philosophy should be such that God can be an object of cognition."

Still another objection comes from those with a high regard for truth who believe that it can not be attained. Thus thirteen teachers believe there is no "sure" road of access to truth, and, as we have seen, a much larger number are convinced there is no "one" road. A few believe that there is no one truth, at all. One economist asserts that "Truth is but a kind of 'regulative' idea giving orientation to our scientific work."

Other problems are cited. One teacher demurs on the ground that the proffered formula discounts the value of "hard, patient thinking," while another reminds us that the road is not always "co-operative."

Despite these and other well-taken comments, however, the statistical record remains impressive: 65 per cent of our teachers accept the formula in its present form, while 24 per cent reject it for reasons such as those we have summarized.

We still must compare the teachers' views concerning access to truth with their theistic positions. The three atheists are unanimous in upholding the statement proposed. The deists are almost equally clear, registering 86 per cent positive and 11 per cent negative. Next in proportion of approval are the theistic naturalists, with 72 per cent for and 14 per cent against. The Pelagians vote 69 per cent for and 21 per cent against, followed by "others" with 60 per cent for and 24 per cent against. The Christocentric group are divided in almost the same proportions, showing 60 per cent for and 29 per cent against.

Thus our familiar curve for these major groups is again broadly confirmed, except that the "other" category is surprisingly close to the Christocentric category. Moreover, the variations in all cases fall slightly short of statistical significance. This reveals that holders of widely differing views of God can sometimes hold a remarkably similar educational concept, even when an issue of religious import is involved in that concept. Evidently the reasons for such divergences are only tangentially related, if at all, to the teachers' particular views of God.

Concerning question 15a, dealing with divine revelation, the trend of correspondence to theistic concept is fairly clear. For simplification, let us note only the forty-three negative replies. They comprise 100 per cent of the atheists, 27 per cent of the philosophical "others," 14 per cent of the theistic naturalists, 11 per cent of the deists, 6 per cent of the Pelagians, and 5 per cent of the Christocentric theists, showing a progressive decrease in the belief in divine revelation the farther we depart from "orthodoxy" in the view of God.

These proportions on the two questions cited are their own best commentary. Where the issue involves a clearly recognizable Christian concept such as divine revelation in question 15a, the answers fall into a clearer pattern than they do where the Christian import of the issue is less visible to the teacher, as in the educational problem concerning the means of access to truth in question 5a. The view of God shows a closer correlation with views in the first area than with views in the second area.

The chief disclosure of these last pages is that on the problem of how to arrive at truth, the majority of the teachers reply differently when the religious bearing is made explicit than they do when it is deeply buried, or perhaps lost, in relation to a particular educational concept. This reveals a basic problem of conceptual dichotomy between religion and education in church-related colleges.

The second area in which we note a contrast between the answers provided to different questions in Table X relates to number 18, dealing with the dangers of disclosing one's Christian view in teaching. Though the teachers have just completed their affirmation of harmony between education and religion, they grow more cautious in appraising the hazards of the wrong use of the classroom. The majority still do not fear the danger. With ratios averaging about three to one, they continue to feel that religion and education can be brought together with impunity, but the drop in the proportions is revealing. They are now warning against possible abuses through the incursion of religion where it does not belong.

In addition to the dangers of sectarianism, dogmatism, obscurantism, and the substitution of piety for sound scholarship, the opposite fear of doing an injustice to Christianity is mentioned by several teachers. One poses the question: "What about the danger of diluting one's Christian beliefs into a sort of wooly ethics?" An economics professor fears the danger of "conventionality," while a colleague in the same field states that the teacher relating his Christian views to his teaching is "in danger to be accused of infringing into the subject matter of the teachers of religious subjects." This is a good illustration of the widespread compartmentalization of thought within the respective fields of the curriculum.

Most of the comments in connection with this question, however, emphasize that there is danger of the qualities listed, but that the danger can be avoided by the right view of Christianity and by the right view and method of teaching. One teacher says, "The answer to this depends very greatly on the professor and on the method of relating his views. If it takes the form of frequent divergences from his own field into that of religion he may be guilty of any or all of the characteristics listed." Another teacher, on the other hand, affirms that "my religion is not in a different field from my subject matter." A third believes that it "depends upon the field of teaching."

A number of our collaborators believe that the dangers of not relating one's Christian views are greater than the dangers of doing so. A teacher with theological training asserts, "I regard such criticism as 'pure rot.' I would rather ask myself, what would Cardinal Newman or Jacques Maritain do?" A sociologist feels that the "error of omission is as bad as the error of commission." An economist sees inevitable danger, "but there is no need to run away. The dangers are greater in the other direction. Students want some guidance, and to understand why we think as we do."

It is of interest how widely the teachers vary on the issue of sectarianism. One avers that there is "possible [danger] if his [the teacher's] Christianity is denominational." Another, on the contrary, believes that the suggested dangers do not exist "in a denominational college."

Several statements on the teacher and his method will give the flavor of a much larger number of comments. A dean of a department of English interjects in answer to the overall question concerning the possible dangers of relating one's Christian view to his teaching: "No; not unless he is a fool or a fanatic." Another English teacher feels that though there are some dangers, the benefits outweigh them if "trivial, controversial issues" are avoided and "broad, fundamental truths applicable to all religious beliefs" are emphasized. One teacher stresses the corrective which is provided by being a "well-rounded intellectual," and another feels it all depends on whether the teacher is "well-educated—liberally trained."

An English professor feels the dangers are very great: "I've seen it happen all too often. The 'relating' becomes quickly direct indoctrination. A college professor (outside of the fields of religion and sociology) who consciously and

regularly tries to teach any one point of view on any subject is in my opinion untrue to the fundamental idea of
'scholarship.' " Finally we quote the statement of a teacher
who believes it is hazardous "only if it constitutes a. bias;
b. gratuitous irreligion; c. superficiality in scientific method
or discipline; or d. exhibitionism." Thus we find, in addition
to the majority of teachers who do not feel the danger, a
strong minority who feel it but do not comment, and an
even larger minority who provide qualified responses.

To test the correspondence of attitude on this question with
the view of God, we take as a sample the replies on the
danger of dogmatism. Here all three of the atheists affirm the
danger. Thirty-six per cent of the theistic naturalists see such
a danger, while 28 per cent do not; 33 per cent of the "philosophical" group fear the danger, while 27 per cent do not;
25 per cent of the deists cite the danger, against 29 per cent
who do not; the Pelagians show 19 per cent yes, 55 per cent
no; the orthodox theists 11 per cent yes, 56 per cent no. We
note a general progression in proportion to the "conservatism" of the view of God.

The third set of contrasts provided in Table X involves
the quotation in 17d. In the large majority of answers to this
question, we have the teachers' reaffirmation that, despite the
intellectual integration that is possible and indeed necessary
between religion and education, the most important facts of
the Christian life have to do with other areas than those of
intellectual abstraction or fixed religious observance.

The comments on this question reveal that the minority
who rejected the statement had three major concerns. The
largest number felt that the formulation should not be so exclusive, as the Christian faith and life involve all the factors
mentioned. The next largest group rejected the statement because it leaves unstated the central belief in salvation through
Christ. Some of them feel that the statement could apply
equally well to other great religions.

An economics teacher puts this position so sharply that it appears exclusive in the other direction: "A 'Christian' means to me a *believer* in the divinity of Christ and his salvation of those who seek redemption from sin." A professor of English, while not specifying what beliefs he has in mind, is equally clear on the primacy of belief. He asserts without reservation, "Acceptance of certain axiomatic beliefs should and must precede religious activity." Another teacher feels that the statement as it stands "looks 'loaded' against formal 'church' Christianity." Still another: "I would regard wide acceptance for this idea as the basic weakness of Christianity."

A third substantial group within the minority are less precise in their formulation of Christianity, but feel that the statement minimizes the place of Jesus as example and inspiration. One says, "A Christian is one who tries as hard as he can to do as he thinks Jesus would do in his position." A similar view is put thus: "What makes a man a Christian is the acceptance of the value system of human relationships emphasized by Jesus." Again, a teacher regards as central the "acceptance of the principles set forth by Christ and the demonstration in one's life of their acceptance."

The position of some of the teachers is even broader. We quote two of them here, because they probably reflect the views of a large number of the majority who answered this question positively and who hence did not comment. One states, "Personally, I like to make 'Christian' synonymous with religious. But I realize that this is not historically correct." The other teacher feels that "What usually makes a man a 'Christian' is that that is what he grew up to call himself!"

On the correspondence of these views with view of God, we record as an indicator simply the forty-four negative replies. Those who do not agree with the statement comprise one of the three atheists, 5 per cent of the theistic naturalists, 7 per cent of the deists, 10 per cent of the Pelagians, 13 per cent of the most conservative theists, and 4 per cent of the "philosophical" group. These proportions, while not strikingly at variance with one another, tend to indicate that some of those who are most conventionally "Christian" in their theism also place the greatest relative importance on ideas and rules, rather than on "a certain spirit and a certain life" as the marks of the Christian.

In summary, the evidence in this section of our report adds up to four findings. First, in the conscious thought of the teacher, the issue of science and religion, or of other educational disciplines and religion, has, on the whole, been resolved, though there are exceptions in the cases of the more religiously conservative faculty members and of certain others at the opposite pole. Second, many of the teachers show inconsistencies and lack of integration between some of their religious views and some of their educational views and practices. Certainly there is no clear correlation between educational concepts and concepts of God. Third, many of the teachers who believe that religion and education should be interrelated nevertheless are warning us that the disclosing of religious beliefs in teaching is fraught with dangers. Finally, a conspicuous majority of the teachers, though they have affirmed elsewhere the importance of seeking to understand and formulate one's religion, believe that the heart of the matter is a man's "possession of a certain spirit and his participation in a certain life."

Religion and the Teacher's Subject

In what ways do the teachers' religious beliefs and practices affect their conception and presentation of the material with which they deal in their respective fields? To avoid undue theorizing, many of the questions in the study were posed in terms of the teacher's own subject rather than on the basis only of general principle. This was designed to make the answers as relevant as possible to actual experience and to provide a basis for comparing the differences from one subject matter area to another.

To what extent, for example, do the teachers in particular departments regard their fields as more relevant or less relevant to religious truth than are other subject-matter fields? Here we divided the teachers not according to the four subjects they teach, as heretofore, but according to the three broad areas of the curriculum which they represent, namely the humanities, the social sciences, and the natural sciences, combining sociology and economics into one group.[15] The replies are worthy of comment.

The English and sociology teachers are clearly the most aware of the religious bearing of their fields. The replies both here and elsewhere in the questionnaires abound with quotations affirming the concern of literature with all of life, including the religious. On our present question, one English teacher presents it as his perspective that "the objectives of education can not be attacked piecemeal. They are all wrapped up in one common objective—to educate the whole man." Another believes that "all truth is religious." One extends himself further: "Literature has, for me, taken the place of organized religion." A fourth, speaking comparatively, holds for English that "mine is a social science more than the 'social sciences.' "

Sixty-six per cent of the English teachers consider religious

---

[15] We should comment here, in anticipation of our next chapter, that there are differences between the prevailing views of sociology teachers and those of economics teachers on important questions in this study. We shall attempt to identify reasons for this at the proper time. Our present concern is to note that the two groups taken together as representatives of the social sciences tend to balance one another off. This probably accounts for the close correspondence of views between the representatives of the humanities and of the social sciences as reported in the following paragraphs. This question was divided on the basis of the three general fields to provide a broad comparative view and to avoid unmanageable and confusing complexity in the interpretation.

truth equally relevant to their field and to the social sciences, but 17 per cent regard it as more relevant and only 6 per cent as less relevant. They are even clearer that religion is more closely related to their field than it is to the physical sciences, only 43 per cent saying equally relevant, while 45 per cent say more relevant, and 3 per cent say less relevant.

The sociologists and economists also believe in the superior religious bearing of their field, though not so strongly as do the English teachers. They show 57 per cent considering their field and the humanities as equally relevant to religion, while 17 per cent regard their field as more relevant, and almost the same number, 15 per cent, believe it less relevant. Similarly, their sense of greater relevance in comparison with the physical sciences is slightly lower than for English teachers, 55 per cent feeling equal relevance, 32 per cent more relevance, and 8 per cent less relevance.

The physics teachers are less convinced of the religious relevance of their field, and show a strikingly equal evaluation of the social sciences and the humanities. The figures for equal relevance are respectively 33 per cent for the social sciences and 31 per cent for the humanities, those believing there is more religious relevance in physics show respectively 19 per cent and 17 per cent, and those feeling less relevance are exactly 36 per cent in relation to both other groups. Thus twice as many physics teachers feel less relevance in their field as those who see more relevance, which reverses the feeling of the teachers in the humanities and social sciences concerning their respective fields.

Making allowances for the natural desire of many teachers to find special religious bearing in their particular fields, and discounting accordingly the number of enthusiasts for "more relevance," it is notable that on the whole the teachers of each group substantiate one another's appraisal of their respective fields. The clearest result, of course, is that physics is regarded by both its own teachers and the other teachers as being significantly less relevant to religion than are the other two fields. This is further borne out, as we shall see, by other evidence in the study.

Perhaps the clearest testimony to the differences of attitude regarding subjects is contained in the replies concerning the religious orientation, if any, of textbooks. While we must bear in mind that many teachers do not select their texts, a fact which a number of them point out, it is nevertheless worth noting that 83 per cent give definite answers to the question and that only 25 per cent report that they consider religious orientation. To provide a clue to differences in this regard from one teaching field to another, we divided the answers according to the four subjects taught.

This breakdown shows 45 per cent of the sociology teachers taking account of the religious orientation of the texts they use and 27 per cent of the English teachers answering similarly. The positive responses by the economics and physics teachers are only 17 per cent and 11 per cent respectively. The difference between sociologists and economists will be analyzed when we consider factors in the teachers' backgrounds. Our present purpose is to observe, in connection with the religious concepts of the teachers, only the specific question as to their sense of the bearing of religious truth upon their respective subject matter fields. The replies disclose significant differences in this regard in accordance with subjects taught. The physics and economics teachers deviate away from a consideration of religious orientation, the sociology teachers deviate in its favor, and the English teachers conform too closely to the averages for the total population of the study to call for separate recording of their ratios.[16]

An examination of the textbooks cited reveals both a lack

16	English Teachers	Sociology Teachers	Economics Teachers	Physics Teachers
CR	—	+3.71	—1.97	—2.83
P	—	.0001	.05	.005

of concentration upon any one work or author regarded as representing a religious orientation, and a scarcity of any books at all in certain fields. The writings in English and sociology clearly and understandably predominate. Thus, of 188 listings (including 26 books cited two or more times), 43 per cent are in the field of English, 34 per cent in sociology, and 7 per cent in economics. An additional 16 per cent do not belong primarily to any one of the four fields in our study, or their identity is not clear from the information given.

The percentage of books in English is lower in ratio to the number of English teachers reporting than is the percentage for sociology in ratio to the number of sociology teachers. The overwhelming majority of titles cited in English are the original works of great writers rather than texts of interpretation. This is in line with the findings of the study conducted by the Hazen Foundation and the American Council on Education. This survey reports, "Professor John H. Roberts, Chairman of the English Department at Williams College, has summed up the matter. In answer to my inquiry, he replied, 'In all our courses we are frequently discussing religious topics, but we do not, I think, use any secondary works specifically on religion.' "[17]

Despite the prevailing situation regarding secondary texts as summarized by Professor Roberts, Professor Spencer is able to cite eight important anthologies in which the religious element in the selected authors is especially emphasized.[18] Only one of these anthologies is mentioned by our responding teachers and this only twice.

In sociology, the percentage of teacher response is higher, the number of books mentioned is proportionately larger, and

---

[17] American Council on Education and Edward W. Hazen Foundation, *College Reading and Religion*, 1948, Chapter VI, "English Literature," by Theodore Spencer, p. 167.

[18] *Ibid.*, p. 176.

a comparison with the listings of books in the Hazen Foundation and American Council study shows duplication of titles in six cases.[19] In economics, the smaller number of books listed corresponds in no case to titles provided in *College Reading and Religion*.[20] In physics, as we have seen, our respondents furnish no titles at all, though again we find in *College Reading and Religion* a substantial listing of works in which the religious element is directly or indirectly treated.[21]

The comments of the respondents on this question are extensive and revealing. They indicate that many teachers consider that their chief religious responsibility in relation to textbooks is not positive but negative, namely to avoid what may be harmful or perhaps unpopular. One teacher writes, "I should not select a text in English literature, for example, written by Jesuits." Some of the teachers carry this approach to the point of eliminating particular chapters in a book otherwise acceptable.

A more common viewpoint is simply that religion is out of place in relation to the particular field. This attitude is expressed by teachers of all four subjects. A closely related position concerns the responsibility of other departments. A sociology teacher answers, "None; our school requires certain religious courses; my books are judged by subject material only." An economist believes that his field is "essentially areligious." Illustrations of this viewpoint could be cited from every field, another evidence of the distinction which many of the teachers draw between religion and their teaching responsibility.

The opposite view is equally frequent, especially in English and sociology. "All good literature is religious." "All

---

[19] *Ibid.*, Chapter X, "Sociology," by Robert L. Sutherland, pp. 263-85.
[20] *Ibid.*, Chapter IX, "Economics," by William A. Orton, pp. 232-62.
[21] *Ibid.*, Chapter XII, "Physical Sciences," by Henry Margenau, pp. 307-23.

literary works of any consequence have underlying philosophical value." A sociologist feels that "Most of the standard texts are satisfactory—or if necessary may be supple-
mented." Another sociologist feels that the religious orientation of texts in his field was better twenty years ago than it
is now.

Even some of the physics teachers, who have been able to
name no texts, feel the inescapable religious orientation of
their subject. One of them states, "A standard text in any
physical science can't help but be a revelation of a Divine or
Supreme Being." Another says, "It is not unthinkable that a
book might appear 'orienting' physics and religion. But it
then would not likely be a physics textbook—perhaps one on
metaphysics." Other physicists who comment point out that
there are at present books in this general field which are not
suitable as texts in undergraduate physics.

A number of teachers in sociology and economics stress the
problem of the diversity of religious viewpoint in our society
as making the religious orientation of texts impracticable. Yet
several of them mention that it is done successfully by the
Roman Catholics. One economics teacher states, "This is a
crying need in a church-related college and Protestants ought
to co-operate to get good, religiously oriented texts published." An English teacher mentions Catholic books in his
field as the only ones of which he appears to be aware which
have a religious orientation.

In short, the experience and viewpoints of the teachers
regarding textbooks are widely diverse. We must note that
the teachers who have made comments constitute only 21 per
cent of the 440 in our survey, and that only 15 per cent of
the teachers cite any books at all which they consider as
having a religious orientation. This apparently is a commentary on the shortage of textbooks of this character. But
since some of the teachers in all four fields except physics
do mention such books, and since we know from such studies

as that by the Hazen Foundation and the American Council on Education that such texts in these subjects exist, the small percentage of replies is also an indication that most of the teachers evidently do not attach as great importance as they might to the religious factor in selecting textbooks.

Our check on views of God discloses that the teachers considering religious orientation in the selection of textbooks include none of the atheists, 31 per cent of the theistic naturalists, 18 per cent of the deists, 24 per cent of the Pelagians, 30 per cent of the more traditional Christians, and 9 per cent of the "philosophers." The proportions are in line *mutatis mutandis* with evidence we shall cite later that the atheists and the "philosophical" group are less concerned with religious orientation in their teaching than are the teachers with more conventional theistic concepts. Among the various more conventional theistic groupings themselves, the differences of response on the textbook issue are not significant.

A further clue to the question of religion in relation to subjects taught is to be found in the teachers' replies concerning the most dependable aids to their own religious growth. We find that 47 per cent of the teachers are helped by "pondering their own subject matter field in its religious bearings." A breakdown of this figure shows the same general progression of the teachers' apparent sense of the relevance of religious truth to their fields, with the English and sociology teachers at the top and the physicists and economists lower down. On this broad question of pondering their subjects in relation to their religious bearings, however, the difference between the teachers of different subjects is not statistically significant.

Dividing the teachers according to their views of God, we find in the replies to this question little difference between the sensitivity of the teachers in different fields to the religious bearings of their subjects. Seventy-two per cent of the theistic naturalists, 48 per cent of the "philosophers," and 48 per cent of the deists check this practice as an aid to religious growth, while only 44 per cent of the Pelagians and 43 per cent of the more Christocentric theists check it. There is a suggestion here that, relative to other religious disciplines, the more orthodox or conventional teachers place slightly less emphasis upon the pondering of their subject matter in its religious bearings than do the teachers who are more liberal theologically. But again the differences statistically are not significant, and we shall need to look elsewhere for better evidence of broad trends in the relation of theistic view to other concepts and to religious practices.

Without transgressing on our next chapter, we may note two replies of the teachers to the question as to where greater stress should be placed in the graduate training of teachers for their respective fields. By far the largest number check a "broader perspective over closely related fields" and "an integration of the subject matter in a total view of human knowledge."

These answers are so interwoven, with 70 per cent checking the first and 74 per cent the second, that we may give the simplest impression of breakdown by analyzing only one. The 325 teachers stressing a total view of human knowledge show a percentage division corresponding closely to the total ratio of teachers in the four subject fields. Again, English is slightly above its total ratio and physics slightly below, but the differences are minimal. The significance of these results lies rather in another direction. They suggest that, though the sense of specific religious orientation differs strongly according to subject fields, the feeling of need for an integration of one's own field with other fields is high among teachers of whatever subject.

Religion and Teaching Practices

We have noted a trend toward dichotomy between religious and educational concepts, and also between religious belief and subject matter content. There is equal evidence of a practical gap between religious beliefs and the disclosure of those beliefs in teaching.

This is especially notable in view of the fact, stated or implied, at many points in the data, that the colleges in overwhelming majority permit the teachers to follow their own judgment in their practice on this matter. Thus in reply to the question, "Do you feel that your institution allows you reasonable freedom in the expression of your views regarding controversial religious issues?" nine-tenths of the teachers said yes, and only 2 per cent registered a definite no. On freedom to discuss controversial social issues, the favorable opinions of the teachers were even more clear, the colleges receiving a clean bill of health from 95 per cent, and a negative judgment from only 1 per cent.

Let us note first the percentages of belief in a particular direction on some central religious issues, and the teachers' replies as to whether they disclose these beliefs in their teaching. We may take as a sample question one we have already examined, which relates religion to education at a crucial point: "Do you believe there are irreconcilable conflicts between the Christian religion as you understand it and some of the findings of science or history in your subject matter field?" We noted previously that only 8 per cent of the teachers answered this question positively. Yet of this group who believe that such a conflict exists, 39 per cent do not make known to their students the point which they feel to be at issue. This illustration is taken from a set of atypical answers, but it is cited because a study of other atypical answers reveals that the teachers who are in small minorities on various issues are particularly reluctant to reveal their views on these issues.

Unwillingness to disclose their beliefs is less marked among the larger number of teachers holding majority views on various questions, but it still is strong. This difference becomes apparent by comparing in table form the percentages of positive and negative beliefs on particular issues with the percentages of persons of these respective beliefs who disclose their views in their teaching.

TABLE XI

COMPARISON OF CERTAIN RELIGIOUS BELIEFS WITH THE TEACHERS'
DISCLOSURE OF THESE BELIEFS IN THEIR TEACHING
(Based on all definite yes and no answers to the indicated
questions averaging 391 answers for each question)

	Positive View			Negative View		
	% Holding This View	% Disclosing View	% Not Disclosing View	% Holding This View	% Disclosing View	% Not Disclosing View
4. Must the conclusions of science and religion ultimately be compatible?[22]	78	85	15	11	61	39
7. Do you regard yourself as a Christian?	94	72	28	2	22	78
9. Is the Bible religiously authoritative?	69	76	24	14	25	75
10. Is church membership necessary to the Christian life?	54	66	34	36	28	72
11. Is prayer necessary to the Christian life?	77	57	43	13	4	96
13. Is man fundamentally good and capable of solving his problems by using his intelligence?	72	78	22	14	31	69
16. Is God the central reality, lending unity to all truth?	77	89	11	6	22	78
17. Do you believe that one must seek an intelligent understanding of his faith?	90	76	24	3	36	64
Average percentages	76	75	25	12	29	71

[22] To save space in this table, the questions are presented in abbreviated form. The full formulations appear in the Questionnaire, Part B.

Three facts stand out in this table. The first is the large discrepancy between the number of teachers holding a particular belief and the number disclosing that belief, regardless of what the belief might be. The second is that those whose views are positive—or perhaps simply conventional —in relation to certain religious questions disclose their views more readily than do those whose answers are negative. The average ratio is 75 per cent to 25 per cent in the former cases and 29 per cent to 71 per cent in the latter cases.[23]

The third observation from these comparisons is that in the areas of belief closely related to intellectual problems of subject matter the teachers are more inclined to disclose their views than in areas more remote from their teaching fields. Thus the gap between belief and disclosure is not so great in questions 4 and 16 as it is in questions 7, 9, 11, and 13. Question 17 is a borderline case, which does not fall strictly in either category.

Let us consider this issue in relation to views of God. Probably the best example is the question which is most inclusive in regard to the point we are discussing: "Do you consciously disclose your basic religious conviction, whatever it may be, in your teaching?" The teachers responding positively are 63 per cent of the total number of teachers, and those responding negatively constitute 26 per cent. The answers for all teachers run as follows: atheists, 100 per cent negative; "philosophers," 55 per cent negative, 29 per cent positive; deists, 36 per cent negative, 54 per cent positive; theistic naturalists, 31 per cent negative, 57 per cent positive; Pela-

---

[23] The statistical deviations represented in these results are so extraordinarily high that they call for presentation. The critical ratio of the difference in proportions of the teachers responding positively and negatively who disclose their views is 19.52; $P = .0000000000?$. In the case of every question, as is obvious from the table, the deviations are in the same direction. Even in the two cases where the variations are least great, namely question 4 and question 17, the results are significant. $CR = 3.28$; $P = .001$ and $CR = 2.70$; $P = .007$.

gians, 25 per cent negative, 65 per cent positive; Christocentric theists, 16 per cent negative, 70 per cent positive. The progression here is clear and significant. It is evident that the persons who are most conventional in their theism are the ones who are most ready to disclose their basic religious views to their students. This confirms the similar tendency which we noted in the last Table that persons with conservative or positive views on certain ancillary religious questions are more ready to disclose those views than are those whose positions are more liberal.

The differences in practice in relation to different types of religious issues is further illustrated by another category of questions. Three-fourths of the teachers derive their concept of the worthfulness of human life and the brotherhood of man from their view of God. Here we did not ask whether they disclosed this fact to their students but whether the view affected their own dealings with their students: does it "increase your encouragement of originality, independence and personal responsibility in your students?" We find that 94 per cent of the teachers crediting God as the source of their view of man also replied that this concept does increase their encouragement of the indicated qualities in their students. This indicates how strongly the teachers replying positively are influenced inwardly by their beliefs, though as we have seen they are reluctant to disclose their basic views outwardly in their teaching.

Only one-tenth of the teachers state definitely that they do not derive their concept of man from their view of God. These include two of the three atheists, 33 per cent of the "philosophers," and 19 per cent of the theistic naturalists, but all other categories are meagerly represented in these negative replies. Sixty per cent of the teachers replying negatively report that their theistic view, whatever it may be, does not help them in encouraging the indicated qualities in their students. This contrasts with the 94 per cent of the positive teachers who do derive such help from their view of God.

There is indication that many of the teachers not only avoid personal identification with a religious position in their teaching, but that they are unready to acknowledge the contributions of religion to their fields. Thus in answer to the question "Do you seek to interpret to students in your teaching some of the insights or disclosures of religion which you believe have a bearing upon your subject matter?" only three-fourths of the teachers respond affirmatively. In many institutions of higher education this would not be surprising, but the gap between this proportion and the much higher proportion of positive belief which we have noted on basic religious questions as well as on questions of the relation of religion to education is a significant discrepancy for church-related colleges. Evidently one-fourth of the teachers are not relating their religious beliefs to the subjects they are teaching.

On the other side, the reluctance of many teachers in these areas may be an indication of their desire to differentiate between authoritarianism and education. The teachers as a whole reveal a sound philosophy of teaching on two questions previously cited which some of the more conservative teachers might have been expected to answer differently. Eighty-seven per cent answer no, and only 4 per cent answer yes to the important question: "Do you encourage students to avoid areas of study which you feel are inimical to their Christian faith?" Even more conclusive are the 90 per cent positive answers as against only 2 per cent negative answers to the question: "Do you allow students to pursue lines of thought and expression which are at variance with your religious views?"

It is well known that in higher education generally the childhood religious views of most students are subjected to severe strain. In many cases, the earlier religious foundations are either repudiated or lost by default, and the student may or may not develop new foundations commensurate with his new horizons. Perhaps our best clue to the sensitivity of teachers to this problem is to be found in their replies to the question: "If the subject matter of your teaching sometimes undermines the religious faith of your students, do you seek to help them reinterpret and reconstruct their faith on a more adequate foundation?" Sixty-five per cent of the teachers answer this question affirmatively. On the other hand, only 8 per cent reply negatively. The remaining 27 per cent either express uncertainty, qualify their answers, or do not answer at all. The large proportion of inconclusive replies is evidence of confusion in the teachers' own minds as to what the true function of their teaching in relation to the religious faith of their students may be. It is not our task here to describe that function, but simply to cite the evidence that there is substantial disagreement and confusion among the teachers concerning the issue.

Let us note some comments which the teachers have made on this last important question. Of thirty teachers making observations, 70 per cent representing all four subjects make the point that their courses do not undermine student faith in the first place. But most of them proceed to say that if it did, they would help their students to a more positive position. Some state that they would do so individually rather than in the classroom.

A sociology professor, reflecting an assumption previously referred to that subjects other than religion have little religious significance, says, "I don't think there is much need [to help students] as there is less need in social science than in religion." An English teacher feels that there is "no time for this, [it is] only incidental." Another teacher of English says that he does not try to reconstruct their faith, "but I point out the traditional lines of evasion or rationalization or retort to the difficulty." Other evidence in this teacher's questionnaire reveals that, in so far as he relates religion to his teaching at all, it is one of his objects to undermine what he regards as its usually false foundations.

Thus there is a wide variety of opinion and practice, but the numerical answers reveal that the great majority of the teachers seek to help their students reinterpret and reconstruct their faith as occasion demands. This is consistent with the evidence elsewhere in the present section of our study that most of the teachers are ready and even eager to help students on religious problems where they recognize such problems to exist and where they are not expected to articulate too specifically their Christian convictions. But the difficulty remains that frequently they do not appear to recognize when and where such problems do exist in relation to their teaching.

Religion and Student Life

Having found a varied attitude toward the disclosure of religious beliefs through actual teaching, what is the record in the area of extracurricular contacts with students? Are the teachers more prone to share their convictions through these informal relationships?

The answer, in brief, depends upon the character of the convictions to which we refer. Where we are dealing with broad areas of character and philosophy of life, the readiness and desire of teachers to be of help is very pronounced. Where, on the other hand, we refer to more specific activities or disciplines pertaining to the nurture and expression of the Christian faith, the teachers are less active and articulate. Some examples may be cited in table form, based on the replies of all the teachers.

We note that questions 1, 3a, and 5a elicit strong affirmative responses, reflecting a deep concern for the wholesome development of students' lives. Questions 2 and 3c, on the other hand, dealing with explicitly "Christian" concepts or practices, show low participation. On question 2, it is of in-

TABLE XII

THE TEACHERS' ATTITUDES TOWARD HELPING STUDENTS RELIGIOUSLY
THROUGH EXTRACURRICULAR CONTACTS

		% Yes	% No	% Uncertain, Qualified, or No Answer
1.	Do you regard it as part of your responsibility in your extracurricular contacts with students to help them develop their Christian character?	82	9	9
2.	Do you seek to assist students in the deepening of their spiritual life through Bible reading, devotional practices, and in other ways?	37	51	12
3a.	Do you regard it as part of your responsibility to assist your students in the selection of a life vocation?	88	5	7
3c.	Do you present this problem as a matter of Christian life commitment?	30	50	20
5a.	Do you regard it as part of your responsibility, if so requested, to aid the Student Christian Association, YMCA, YWCA, denominational foundation, or other voluntary student-faculty religious group on your campus?	83	9	8

terest that, whereas we found 77 per cent of the teachers considering prayer as necessary to the Christian life, only 37 per cent "assist students in the deepening of their spiritual life" either through this means or in other ways.

In the matter of helping students choose a vocation, the participation of teachers is high, with 93 per cent assisting at least some students and 40 per cent assisting half or more of their students. Thus the 30 per cent indicated above who present this problem as a matter of Christian life commitment represents less than one-third of the teachers who are counseling students in this area. Here again is indication of their hesitation to articulate their practice, like their concepts, in what they regard as specifically Christian terms.

On the other hand, most of the teachers expressing an opinion in the matter feel that their religious concepts and practices make the attainment of a sense of community with students more easy rather than more difficult, and practically all of them feel that their religion makes these contacts more fruitful than they would otherwise be. Thus according to their own testimony, the possession of their religious convictions is on the whole advantageous to them in their student relationships.

This being true, do the teachers consider that their opportunity to exert a religious influence upon students is greater through extracurricular or through academic contacts? Opinion here is equally divided among four groups: those selecting one or the other of the two types of contact, those saying that the two types of opportunity are equally great, and those saying that they can not be compared.

The range of opportunities outside the classroom is wide. The largest number of teachers feel that they can exert the greatest religious influence through personal counseling, closely followed by those stressing informal, unplanned contacts. Equal to the last group are the group who believe that the greatest opportunity lies in extracurricular activities other than those associated primarily with religious purposes, further confirming the impression that the teachers rely heavily on approaches which are not branded as "Christian." However, all except 2 per cent of the group who checked nonreligious activities checked religious activities as well, which indicates that they do not intend to discount religious approaches.

In the middle range of emphasis are such activities as serving as faculty adviser, entertaining students in the teacher's home, and speaking to meetings. The teachers feel they are able to exert far less, though some, influence through leading in worship, participating in service projects, assisting in the planning of student religious activities, leading Bible study, preaching, and leading other groups.

Distinguished from the activities which the teachers report

as most effective, we note those in which they are requested by campus religious societies to engage. By far the most frequent activity is the giving of talks. Next in line are committee meetings and leading discussions. Thus the services which the teachers are most often invited by the student-faculty religious organizations to render are not the ones in which they feel that they are able to exert the greatest religious influence.

The next most frequent activities are serving as faculty adviser, participating in worship services, using one's home for student religious meetings, helping students relate their Christian convictions to campus problems, assisting in program planning, and assisting in religious emphasis weeks. Some of this middle group of activities correspond more closely to what the teachers feel is effective.

Down the line are numerous activities which we need not recapitulate. It is of interest that 26 per cent sometimes lead worship services, and 13 per cent or less lead Bible study, counsel or train students in religious leadership, or accompany students on deputation teams. Once more our familiar refrain concerning the infrequency of faculty leadership in specifically "religious" activity. There is a correspondence here between the teachers' conviction of their ineffectiveness in these areas and the infrequency with which they evidently are called upon for such help.

We have noted previously the division of the teachers' work load and voluntary extracurricular activities in terms of the number of hours involved per week. Only one-tenth of the teachers state that they devote no time to broadly religious activities such as those we have been discussing, and the median figure, in round numbers, is two hours per week. Less than a fifth of the teachers in the study indicate that they do such work as a responsibility officially assigned by the administration. Thus the amount of time being given voluntarily to assist students in their broadly religious activities may be considered, in light of the heavy faculty work load, as evidence of very genuine interest on the part of the teachers.

Finally, what do our collaborators regard as the desirable lines of purpose and program for the voluntary student-faculty religious organization on the campus? Only one-tenth of them believe this group should be distinctly Christian in the three basic characteristics of purpose, program, and membership. One-half, however, believe it should be Christian in purpose and program but inclusive in membership, which is the pattern of most existing Student Christian Associations, Y.M.C.A.'s and Y.W.C.A.'s on college campuses. Thirty per cent believe such a group should be inclusively interfaith in character.

Consistent with these views is the overwhelming preference for nondenominational as against denominational student religious programs on the campuses. The vote for the former is more than eight times that of the latter, despite the clear loyalty to their respective denominations which many of the teachers reveal in other connections.

The evidence, in short, begins to present a pattern. As in teaching practices, so in extracurricular student contacts, the teachers on the whole have shown a broad and deep religious concern and in most cases a definite Christian conviction. They give extracurricular leadership generously in general religious directions, but large numbers are reluctant for one reason or another to give full expression to specific Christian views or to propagate these views among their students. The majority of the teachers also express in manifold ways their fear of sectarianism and narrow denominationalism, and in many cases they appear to fear that specific Christian activities such as prayer and Bible study are subject to the sin of narrowness.

Moreover, we find here as elsewhere that certain views and activities appear to bear a relation to concepts of God, and certain others do not. On the development of Christian char-

acter in their students, only thirty-eight teachers reply negatively. They embrace two of the three atheists and more than
a fourth of the "philosophers" but only insignificant proportions of all other categories. The total replies on assisting
students in the "deepening of their spiritual life" are more
evenly divided with a third yes and a half no; but again there
is a broad correspondence of views with particular views of
God. All three of the atheists are negative, two-thirds of the
"philosophers," theistic naturalists, and deists are negative
while the Pelagians are evenly divided and the Christocentric
theists show a clear majority positive.

On the other hand, the correspondence with views of God
is not borne out when we reach concrete questions with a less
immediate religious bearing. Thus the small group of twenty-four teachers who do not consider it as part of their responsibility to assist their students in the selection of a life
vocation include none of the three atheists and only one of
the "philosophers," while the remaining twenty-three teachers
are drawn chiefly from the Christocentric theists. Similarly
question 4a, asking how the teacher's religious concepts and
practices affect the "attainment of a sense of community with
students," produces only one "philosopher" but eight Christocentric theists, who say "more difficult."

But in question 5a, where we re-enter the religious field,
the prevailing correspondence also re-enters. Thirty-nine
teachers do not consider it a part of their responsibility to
help the Student Y.M.C.A., Y.W.C.A., and other voluntary
religious groups. Two of the three atheists and 18 per cent of
the "philosophers" are in this category. But it embraces only
4 per cent of the Christocentric theists. The correspondence
is similarly clear among the minority of the teachers who believe that the major emphasis should be placed upon denominational rather than nondenominational student religious
programs. The forty-five respondents who prefer the denominational approach include 14 per cent of the Christocentric

group, 9 per cent of the Pelagians, 7 per cent of the deists, 5 per cent of the theistic naturalists, 4 per cent of the "philosophers," and none of the atheists.

Thus as the evidence multiplies, the view of God becomes a reliable index to what we may expect the teachers to believe and even to do in specifically religious areas. But we have found no consistent correlation with concepts and practices in areas which they do not consider religious. Attitudes on nonreligious issues do not fall automatically into line with the conception of divinity, but are conditioned by numerous other factors some of which we shall seek to explore in the next chapter.

Religion and the College

An important element of the teacher's religion in relation to his work is its applications to the institution in which his life is set. How do his religious concepts help to mould his views as to what the college should be, and how do they affect his participation in the common life of the institution?

We have observed previously that the majority of the teachers appear to be happy in their present locations and that they clearly are committed to the church-related college as the type of institution in which they desire to serve. We have also noted that practically all of them consider that the degree of freedom which they are granted in their teaching, on both social and religious issues, is satisfactory. Nor is there evidence of malaise on the part of the teachers with respect to their security in their positions.

The teachers in the main are also in fundamental agreement with the underlying educational philosophies of their institutions. Not only do three-fourths of them believe that God is "the central reality underlying and lending unity to all truth," but the same number believe that the educational philosophy of their institutions is based on this concept, while only 5 per cent assert that this is not its philosophy.

Fortunate is the teacher whose point of departure for his basic conception of truth conforms so closely to that of the institution in which he teaches.

Furthermore, three-fourths of the teachers feel that their administrations make a serious effort to disclose their underlying philosophy in this regard to the students and only one-tenth clearly believe that they do not do so. From twenty-two institutions we get both yes and no answers, and from two institutions we receive only negative answers. This means that in forty-nine of the seventy-three institutions there is full agreement among the replying teachers that their administrations make a genuine attempt to interpret their philosophy on this fundamental point.

Among the teachers who do not think this is the educational philosophies of their colleges, a number attempt to state the philosophy they feel their institutions do represent. There is nothing of great moment in these descriptions, except in the negative sense that they add up to a picture of confusion. We must remember, however, that the teachers expressing these views are but a small minority of the total.

Considerable thought has been given in recent years to the conception of the college or university as an institution in which the faculty members seek to be a closely knit Christian community or "collegium" engaged together in the enterprise of learning and teaching for the glory of God through devotion to his truth. Do the teachers we are discussing feel that the faculties in their institutions should strive toward this end? That the concept is far from general acceptance is suggested by the response, in which one-half gave assent, one-quarter were negative, and one-quarter either did not answer or answered inconclusively. Regardless of their own estimate of this concept, only one-third of the teachers felt that the faculties in their institutions do so regard themselves, but one-half report that such an idea is discussed sometimes in official sessions of the faculty or in committees.

We are dealing here with an intangible but profound concept which involves the essence of the Christian life as a life of shared community. Though this particular view apparently has not penetrated deeply into the consciousness of half of the teachers or of the corporate life of the colleges as a whole, most of the teachers do not attribute this lack to any serious morale problem within the faculty. To the question as to whether "the element of professional rivalry or jealousy among faculty members seriously hinders the realization of such a community in your institution," less than one-fifth say yes, while two-thirds say no.

This exculpation of their colleagues by the majority of the teachers conforms with other evidence in the study, drawn particularly from the final discursive material, that the element of faculty friction appears to have a remarkably low place as a major problem in the consciousness of the teachers. It also suggests that the reason the "collegium" idea does not have a firmer hold is not so much that the climate of intrafaculty human relationships would be unfavorable to it, but rather that the idea has not taken deep root conceptually.

A closely related question is whether the teachers believe the college should select the members of its faculty with a view to their religious beliefs. This issue was couched in a succession of five statements on each of which the reactions of the teachers were solicited. The results for all the teachers are presented in Table XIII.

These questions are not mutually exclusive. Broadly speaking, they represent a progression from the most specific to the most general religious requirements. The middle position, calling for Christian character and conviction, has by far the clearest majority, and the proportions taper off from this to negative majorities at the two extremes of doctrinal requirements on the one side and unspecified religious concern on the other side. The majority for the middle position would probably be even larger, except for the fact that some of the

TABLE XIII

ATTITUDES REGARDING RELIGIOUS REQUIREMENTS FOR SELECTION OF FACULTY

	% Yes	% No	% Uncertain, Qualified, or No Answer
Do you believe that your institution should require its faculty members:			
1. To subscribe to a specific statement of Christian belief before being employed?	21	64	15
2. To be members of an evangelical church?	27	56	17
3. To be Christian in character and conviction?	70	16	14
4. To possess religious conviction, whether Christian or otherwise?	50	21	29
5. To indicate in some other way their religious orientation?	18	23	59

teachers who voted positively on the more conservative options apparently did not understand that they were to express a judgment on each possibility. Presumably they would have voted affirmatively, certainly not negatively, on the third position.

Thus again we find a prevailing Christian conviction, identifying itself as more specifically Christian than merely a broad and unformed religiosity, yet rejecting on the whole the doctrinal test of its authenticity. Not only are the teachers themselves chiefly of this stamp, but they believe that their colleges should be similarly oriented in the selection of faculty members.

The replies to this question provide further evidence of correspondence with views of God. The seventy-two teachers stating that the college should not require its teachers to be Christian in character and conviction embrace all of the atheists, 36 per cent of the "philosophers," 25 per cent of the theistic naturalists, 21 per cent of the deists, 13 per cent of the Pelagians, and 9 per cent of the Christocentric theists. We should note, as we have on previous questions, that this instance of clear correlation is on another specifically religious issue.

In harmony with the prevailing view of the teachers on this question is the reluctance of most of them to take issue with the college authorities on these matters. Only 13 per cent state that they usually inform the administration when they disagree with its position on religious questions, while 24 per cent say that they sometimes do, and 43 per cent say that they never do. It is even more striking that only two of the 440 teachers, or less than one-half of one per cent, report that they usually inform the administration of nonconformity in the religious views of faculty colleagues, while only 6 per cent sometimes do, and 85 per cent never do. If, as is sometimes charged, the colleges are subjected to "witch hunts" on matters of religious doctrine, we have here ample evidence that within the scope of our sampling the hunters are not to be found among the teachers.

Similarly, the majority of the teachers do not believe that their institutions should require chapel attendance on the part of faculty members, and a substantial minority do not believe that it should be required of students. The teachers from the institutions in which student chapel attendance is not required are almost unanimous in their rejection of compulsory chapel for both students and faculty.

Lest chapel attendance be regarded as the chief criterion of administration policy on religion, we asked whether the institution should require any other religious activities on the part of either students or faculty members. The response was almost equally negative with reference to both students and teachers, the proportions opposing such requirements being approximately six to one in the case of both groups.

There is an almost even division of opinion as to whether the institution, "if it has made clear to prospective students its position on religious matters, should select its students partly on religious grounds." The answers do not conform to any clear patterns in relation to theistic concept, indicating again that the view of God does not predetermine the views on educational philosophy and practice, even where a religious issue is clearly involved.

On another matter of college policy, however, the teachers present a more united verdict. Two-thirds of the responders believe the institution's religious policy and practice should be determined co-operatively by the administration, the faculty, and the students, while one-fifth believe this is the task of the administration and the faculty without the students, and only one-tenth believe it is the responsibility of the administration alone.

The teachers are not so sure that the procedures they favor in this regard are the ones which are practiced. Only one-third feel that the religious policy of their institutions is determined in the manner that two-thirds desire, namely by administration, faculty, and students co-operatively. One-fifth say it is determined by administration and faculty, which is closely in line with the number desiring this procedure, but one-fifth report that it is determined by the administration alone, as against the one-tenth who approve this procedure.

In view of the conviction of the teachers in this area, it is of interest that only one-fifth of them have served on co-operative committees to deal with the problem, whereas one-half would like to serve on such a committee if requested to do so, and only one-fifth state that they would prefer not to serve on such a committee. Thus a large proportion of the teachers desire a greater share in the determination of college policy than they at present enjoy.

We shall note presently the opinions of the teachers concerning the policies of their institutions on certain social issues in which the college is necessarily involved. These concern areas in which the individual social judgment of the teachers might be reflected. We may note here their views on the broader question of college policy, finding that nine-tenths "regard it as one of the functions of their institutions to help shape the character of the social order in the direction of greater justice; if necessary, at the risk of public criticism." Yet only three-fifths believe that their institutions regard this to be one of their functions. It is not surprising, nor a refutation of evidence we shall cite concerning the social moderation of the teachers, to find that many of them consider their colleges less aggressive in this regard than the teachers feel they ought to be.

A further problem which is much in the consciousness of church-related colleges is that of secularization. To sound out the teachers on this issue, we asked the following question: "Do you believe that the present degree of secularization in your college is, on the whole, a healthy condition for a Christian institution of higher education in view of the secularization of the society from which the students are drawn and to which they will return?" The diversity of opinion and the uncertainty in the teachers' minds is evidenced by a 39 per cent yes reply, 26 per cent no, and 26 per cent uncertain.

It must be recognized that the issue of secularization of college life is peculiarly complicated and does not lend itself as readily as do most of the questions to clear yes or no answers. One indication of this is that several of the persons responding negatively do so not because they think their colleges are too secular but because they do not think they are secular enough. Moreover, the answers to this question depend not only upon the orientation of the teacher, which is our chief concern in this study, but upon the degree of secularization in his particular institution. Presumably the same teacher who answers the question positively in relation to the school in which he is now situated might answer it negatively in relation to another institution.

There is similar division of judgment as to whether college life is more secular or less secular than it was ten years ago. The question was posed with regard to the outlooks of students, of faculty members, and of administrations. For each category, approximately one-fourth of the teachers expressed uncertainty. But the largest single group in each instance, representing 27 per cent for students, 30 per cent for faculty, and 38 per cent for the administration, felt that the degree of secularization has not greatly changed in the last decade. Approximately two teachers believe there is greater secularization in their colleges for every one teacher who believes there is less, but even so, the number of teachers who believe it is greater in no case exceeds one-fourth of the 440 respondents.

The best source in this study for the teachers' broad opinions on the church-related colleges, in addition to the evidence heretofore cited, is the set of answers to the questions calling for the wording of replies by the respondents themselves regarding their institutions. This extensive material has been organized and classified in the full report of the survey. The chief data, however, may be recapitulated here.

Let us take only the question which asks for "the measures most needed in your college to develop a sound and effective Christian higher education." The length of the list of answers provided by 260 teachers may appear formidable, but as much combining has been done as was possible without violating intended meanings or omitting special ideas which add richness and color to the total data. To secure a yardstick of frequency, we set a dividing line between those listings which aggregate 2 per cent or more of the total of 577 measures suggested, and those which aggregate less than 2 per cent. Scrutiny of the items above and below this line reveals that, taking all the relevant areas together, this division gives us an accurate grouping of the items which the teachers considered most important. Hence only those aggregating as much as 2 per cent of the total are included in the table.

The information in Table XIV calls for little amplification. Perhaps its chief disclosure is negative: the absence of any

TABLE XIV

THE TEACHERS' LISTINGS OF THE CHIEF MEASURES NEEDED IN
CHURCH-RELATED COLLEGES
(Based on a total of 577 listings)

	% of Total Listings
A. *Faculty Measures:*	
1. Faculty *qualifications:*	
a. Deeper Christian conviction	6
b. Greater all-round ability	2
c. Greater ability as teachers	2
2. Faculty *practices:*	
a. A better blend of Christianity with teaching	4
b. More Christian example, less theory	3
c. Greater concern for total life of students	2
d. More faculty religious fellowship	2
3. Faculty treatment by *college:*	
a. Improved salaries, tenure, security	2
b. Reduced work load	2
B. *Philosophy of Education:*	
1. Better understanding of Christian function of college	4
2. Better integration of religion in the curriculum	3
3. More broad-mindedness in religious outlook	2
C. *Finance and Facilities:* (In addition to faculty salaries, etc., recorded above)	
1. Improved physical plant and total financial position of college	3
D. *College Control:*	
1. More courageously Christian administration	3
2. More able and responsible administration	2
3. More democracy, liberalism and faculty participation in determining college policy	2
E. *College Life (general):*	
1. More student-faculty contact and co-operation	3
2. Better counseling program	2
F. *College Religious Life:*	
1. Better quality in overall religious program	5
2. More contact of religion with life	2
3. More worshipful chapel	2
G. *Relation of College to Society:* (None above 1 per cent)	
H. *Student Issues:*	
1. Recruit abler students	2
2. Better interpretation to students of college opportunity and requirements	2

unified, commanding concern which could be interpreted as
a clear consensus of the teachers regarding the basic needs

of Christian higher education. There is little evidence here of strong movements of thought on the issues at stake, sweeping the colleges in a common direction. This lack could be discounted if it were observed only on this one question, but it conforms to the evidence of the study as a whole.

The net impression from these comments may be one of undue criticism and even dissatisfaction on the part of the teachers. But we specifically requested proposals for improvement, and we have noted elsewhere the prevailing contentment of the teachers in their positions. Thus the present data may be regarded on the whole not as the censure of detractors, but as the honest analysis of the colleges by loyal and responsible friends who desire even greater strength in their institutions.

In broad outline, the comments which we have summarized in the preceding table, and the more detailed material from which they come, are in line with the data we have cited and sought to interpret throughout this chapter. The present material complements our preceding analysis by eliciting suggestions which the earlier question and answer procedure could not produce. But the suggestions do not add up to any faculty manifesto. In the sections of the next chapter dealing with training we shall seek a fuller understanding of the teachers' views.

Religion and Social Issues

Proceeding from the general to the more specific, we have presented the teachers' religious concepts *per se;* we have analyzed them in relation to educational philosophy; and we have related them to the respective teaching fields. We then examined them as applied to teaching practices, to student contacts, and to the life of the college. We shall now inquire how the teachers relate their religious views to concrete social issues.

Our collaborators' self-appraisal here appears to be

favorable. They report that they take the social implications of their teaching with due seriousness. Thus 90 per cent of the teachers "believe that the pursuit of truth in their subject matter fields carries an obligation to relate that truth to the social order," and 88 per cent "relate the truth in their fields to contemporary social problems, even on controversial issues." Applying the same philosophy to their colleges, we have noted that nine-tenths "regard it as one of the functions of their institutions to help shape the character of the social order in the direction of greater justice; if necessary, at the risk of public criticism."

The distribution on views of God in relation to each of the three questions stated reveals no significant differences in basic attitude toward social responsibility among the several theistic classifications. This is not surprising in view of the small total number of persons, regardless of classification, who answered negatively.

These professions of social interest do not appear to be fully borne out by other evidence in the study. At the points where opportunity was given the teachers to say whatever was most in their hearts to say, there is little expression of social concern. After making allowance for the fact that this may appear as a tangential interest in relation to religion and higher education, and for this reason may not have been stressed in the replies, the fact remains that its absence is conspicuous.

A case in point is the question on "the religious activities or problems with which you find yourself least able to deal in the course of your work." Despite the fact that a third of our teachers are in the social sciences, the references to the relation between religious problems and social issues comprise a bare 3 per cent of the total problems and activities cited. Moreover, these particular references add up to what we have summarized in our background data as "confusion or timidity on social issues." There are an additional fifteen references, or 3 per cent, to the failure on the part of students to see the social implications of Christianity, and three references, or 1 per cent, to the problem of race as it relates to students.

Again, in listing "the chief weaknesses of church-related colleges as you have experienced them," we get the following responses with a specifically social bearing: policy of college determined by money interests, four references; college too aloof from social issues, four references; faculty untrained in social sciences, three references; no application of education to society, three references; hopelessness about Christian social objectives, two references; "ethnocentrism (racial, geographical, denominational, etc.)," one reference. This totals seventeen references, or 3 per cent, out of 675 listings in reply to this question.

Coming at the matter positively, as already noted, we asked for "the chief measures needed in your college to develop a sound and effective Christian higher education." Of the total number of 577 suggestions, only twelve, or 2 per cent, could be considered in a genuine sense as reflecting a consciousness of the college's direct responsibility for training students to cope with social issues.

As a final illustration, we cite the responses to our request for comments on a separate sheet concerning "whatever you would most like to say regarding the college teacher's relation to religion in higher education, with special reference to training." This admittedly is an area which one would not associate immediately with social issues, but it is safe to say that if burning social convictions had been moving in the hearts of many of the teachers, some of them would have come to expression. Yet, out of 165 discursive offerings on separate sheets, there were only six references, or 4 per cent, to social questions. Two teachers declared that church-related colleges are backward on social issues; one asserted the need for Christian-oriented sociology textbooks; one stated that there is no "Christian" sociology but only Christian teachers of sociology; one said that more Jews should be admitted to the student body; and one advocated employing qualified Negroes on the faculty. These six comments reflect sensitivity to social issues in relation to religion in higher education, but they are very few in number.

Even if we had found a vibrant social consciousness, we still would have to analyze the direction in which it pointed. It would be both presumptuous and a digression from our main purpose in this study to pass judgment on the social views of our teachers. It is important, however, for us to know what the teachers think on certain issues of this kind, and how their social convictions relate to their theology.

Response by 97 per cent of the teachers indicated deep interest in the question: "Do you believe that under existing conditions your institution should select its prospective students partly on grounds of race, color, or national origin?" The direction of the interest, however, was sharply divided. Two-thirds of those answering said yes and one-third said no.

The division of opinion is reflected in the teachers' comments. One teacher, who calls himself an agnostic and in many other respects is a nonconformist, is vehement in his response: "No! This is true for most American colleges and universities, and is most shameful." Some of the answers which we have had to call qualified stress the phrase "under existing conditions" as including state laws, and thus justify the advocacy of segregation, but affirm their belief in an ultimate goal of nonsegregation. This applies particularly to teachers in the South, who constitute, as we shall see later, a disproportionate number of the "positive" answers to this question.

A dean who states that it is "obviously impractical to include Negroes in a southern school" hastens to assure us that "we enroll Hawaiian, Chinese, and Japanese students." There are numerous poignant expressions of the conflict between the desirable and the possible.

That the problem of race is not exclusively southern is suggested by the statement of a northern teacher that great caution must be exercised, and by another who points to a "dozen foreign students" in his college, but to no Negroes. Teachers of certain other northern schools go out of their way to affirm their institutions' policies of nonsegregation against Negroes or any other group.

There is difference of report from some sections on the actual facts. From Texas, a teacher states that his college "has never refused entrance to a student on any of these grounds, I feel sure." Yet from another institution in the same state a teacher upholds segregation under existing conditions "only because I don't believe our Board or endowment would make it possible to admit Negroes. I'm afraid Texas 'Christian' colleges will be the last to do this."

On a different facet of the issue, a teacher in a northern institution does not want limitations or quotas, and makes clear that he is not a Jew. Yet he returns a yes answer "if this means, should the college positively try to get people of other than Protestant Anglo-Saxon groups."

Of interest here is the division of yes and no answers in relation to the teachers' views of God. The proportions are as follows: atheists, 33 per cent yes, 67 per cent no; theistic naturalists, 26 per cent yes, 62 per cent no; deists, 46 per cent yes, 50 per cent no; Pelagians, 35 per cent yes, 55 per cent no; Christocentric, 31 per cent yes, 62 per cent no; "philosophers," 11 per cent yes, 69 per cent no. Most of the variations here are not statistically significant, but it is worthy of note that the "philosophers" group depart from the general norm, showing a marked racial liberalism in comparison with the others.[24] This is partly, though by no means

---

[24] CR $= 2.74$; P $= .006$.

entirely, accounted for by the fact that few of this group are from the South.

Of even greater interest to the teachers, with a 98 per cent response, was the question: "Do you feel that your institution makes as great an effort as it should under existing circumstances to recruit qualified students from the lower economic and social levels of society?" The judgment of the teachers is 63 per cent positive and 20 per cent negative, with the high proportion of 15 per cent being undecided. It is difficult to assess this response. Those who answered positively may reflect either a healthy admissions policy and practice on the part of their colleges or personal complacency concerning the issue.[25]

Three facts would suggest that the positive response is a further indication of limited social vision on the part of some of the teachers. The first fact is that this interpretation conforms with the other evidence we have adduced that the teacher's theoretical social philosophy is not always translated into pressing social concern or direct social action.

Second, the fact that as many as 20 per cent of the teachers do express dissatisfaction, and that an additional 15 per cent give qualified answers, suggests that there is ground for such dissatisfaction but that the majority of the teachers do not sense it. An analysis of the replies reveals that only six institutions, representing thirty-one teachers, receive a unanimous positive report. Thus there is disagreement regarding the adequacy of institutional policy on this issue in nine-tenths of the colleges, representing the same proportion of the teachers. If it be argued that the minority may be seeing

---

[25] It is well known, of course, that the tuitions and other fees which most church-related institutions are obliged to charge in order to try to keep solvent make it impossible for many students of the lower income groups to attend. A separate study of this question for all the colleges in our survey would be in order. This would focus, however, upon the institutions rather than upon the teachers, who are our present concern.

problems which do not exist, we need only cite the evidence throughout the study that the teachers appear to be scrupulously fair in their evaluations of the policies of their colleges, and scarcely would criticize them at this point if they did not have grounds for doing so.

The third fact is the comments offered by some of the teachers. They furnish evidence that the policies and practices of certain colleges on this issue are not what they should be—or what in fairness the administrations in many cases would like them to be. This fact subjects to further question the social awareness of the majority of the teachers, who report that their colleges are making as great an effort as they should in regard to this issue.

One teacher describes a condition which appears to be typical: "Most of our students are from nonwealthy middle-class families." Another asserts, "There would have to be scholarships for the economically depressed, and there are none as such." A teacher from a very poor school believes that "a considerable effort is made to help. One's answer depends on how high one raises one's objectives."

In this last comment is contained a reason for caution in our conclusions on this issue. While the great majority of the teachers believe that their institutions are making as great an effort as they should to recruit qualified students from the lower economic and social levels of society, the question is relative, because both the "objectives" of the teacher and the practices of the institution are involved. But however this may be, the answers reveal that the teachers who are clearly satisfied are three times as numerous as those who are clearly dissatisfied. This ratio, in light of the other facts we have cited, appears to corroborate our impression of social conservatism on the part of most of our teachers.

On a closely related issue, we discover that one-third of the teachers definitely do not "participate personally in the leadership of political or social affairs" in their communities. This is much higher than the 10 per cent who, as we have noted previously, do not participate in the work of their respective churches.

In short, our data indicate that many of the teachers are conceptually aware of the relevance of both their religion and their subject matter to social issues, but that the practical implications of these concepts are not always so clear in their thought. Nor do most of the teachers give evidence of profound personal concern issuing either in activity which they report or in the suggestion of measures to make Christian higher education more effective in the social sphere.

In this chapter we have attempted to analyze the teachers' basic religious beliefs; we have encountered a frequent separation of their religious concepts from their educational concepts; we have noted varying attitudes to their subject matter in its religious bearings; we have observed a substantial gap between religious belief and the readiness to disclose that belief in teaching; we have indicated the greater readiness of the teachers to deal religiously with students in extracurricular contacts than in academic contacts; we have presented their views on the religious and institutional life of their colleges; and we have discovered an uneven carryover from religious conviction to social conviction.

We now are ready to examine certain background factors for possible correspondence between these factors and the teachers' religious, educational, and social views. We shall also probe their own opinions regarding their personal training experience and that which they desire for the teachers who are to come after them.

4.

FACULTY PREPARATION: FORMATIVE FACTORS IN THE TEACHER'S BACKGROUND

THE TEACHER or administrator reading the foregoing analysis will draw his own inferences from the facts. Disclosures which will be welcomed by one may be received with dismay by another. No reader can fail to be distressed at certain revelations, though the direction of his particular concern may be exactly opposite to that of another reader. Every thoughtful student of higher education will see points at which he desires improvements from his particular point of view.

How are such improvements to be effected? The focus of this study is upon the teacher, not upon the institution. If we desire what we consider to be a more adequate religious orientation and practice on the part of the teachers in our church-related colleges, what can we do to this end? Can present teachers be helped by further in-service training? Shall prospective teachers be differently trained than in the past? Are there factors of personal background or other early influence which in the future could be affected by purposive conditioning? Is there need for better recruiting, or perhaps for the beginning of training of potential teachers at a younger age than the college usually reaches? In what ways can the college, the church, and the home make a concerted religious impact which will help to integrate the insights of education and the insights of religion as part of an over-arching philosophy of Christian education?

106

These are far-reaching and difficult questions. They can not be answered in this book or in any other book. They must be hammered out, as in the past, in continuing years of search and discovery. As previously stated, the object of this study is to furnish facts. We shall examine now certain background influences which may show some indicative correspondence with the teachers' beliefs and practices. If we find clues to present outlook in the timing of religious decisions, in denominational influence, in the type of undergraduate colleges attended, in geographical setting, in specific academic training, in the influence of subject matter, faculty status, or other environing conditions, the statesmen of Christian higher education and the teachers themselves may have new evidence to utilize in seeking to mould the future.

Periods of Greatest Religious Growth

It is a commonplace that a person's general religious orientation usually is determined in the years of his childhood and youth. The length of this formative period varies from case to case, and there are occasional striking changes, of course, after maturity. There is difference of opinion and experience as to how important the college years may be for basic religious development and whether the changes at this time are fundamental or are minor modifications in patterns already well established.

The most exhaustive study which has been made in this area, edited by Hugh Hartshorne, would appear to indicate that changes in other aspects of emotional and character pattern during the college period are inextricably interwoven with the changes in religious orientation.[26] Certainly it can not be claimed on the basis of the evidence in that survey

---

[26] Hartshorne, Hugh, Ed., Lincoln B. Hale et al, *From School to College, A Study of the Transition Experience*. New Haven: Published for the Institute of Social and Religious Research, by the Yale University Press, 1933.

that the religious factor is the dominant one in the determination of personality and character configurations at this stage of life.

In our study of college teachers, we have asked each responder to indicate "the period in your life to which you attribute the greatest importance in the development of the concept or practice to which the question refers." The periods offered for checking were precollege, college, graduate, and the period since completing graduate work.

Beyond the question of period, it was important to discover the character of the broad formative influence to which the teacher attributes the view which he holds on a particular question. We asked "whether the major influence in the development of the concept or practice was your academic work (including the influence of school or college factors outside the classroom) or other influences not directly related to your formal education."

While the proportion of answers to these two questions was somewhat lower than on the basic questions of concept and practice, it still was a large majority. Whereas the "Basic Answers" on the 22 questions involved in this section averaged a 95 per cent response, the average response on "Most Important Period" was 77 per cent and on "Major Influence" was 71 per cent. Thus this device yielded representative and extensive information. It can, however, be quickly summarized.

Averaging the answers to all of the questions on Most Important Period, we reach the following totals: precollege, 32 per cent of the total replying; college, 29 per cent; graduate, 19 per cent; since graduation, 20 per cent. Averaging all of the answers for Major Influence, the results are as follows: academic, 38 per cent of the total replying; nonacademic, 62 per cent of the total replying.

These averages are of significance in themselves, as they indicate the appreciable predominance of the precollege and college periods, and the even stronger predominance of non-academic as against academic influence. The figures assume more meaning when broken down into types of questions. The differences are especially striking between areas which are primarily religious, though with an intellectual bearing, and questions which are primarily intellectual, though with a religious bearing. The summary results are presented in the following table.

TABLE XV

COMPARISON OF PERIOD AND INFLUENCE ON PRIMARILY INTELLECTUAL
AND PRIMARILY RELIGIOUS QUESTIONS

	Most Important Period[27]				Marginal Totals
	P	C	G	S	
	%	%	%	%	
10 primarily intellectual questions	15	34	27	24	3372
7 primarily religious questions	58	19	9	14	2384
3 border-line questions	30	36	14	20	1005
Total					6761

	Major Influence		Marginal Totals
	A	O	
	%	%	
10 primarily intellectual questions	53	47	3098
7 primarily religious questions	17	83	2270
3 border-line questions	43	57	908
Total			6276

The discrepancies revealed in this table are so extraordinarily high that we tested not only the totals according to the three categories but the deviations within the component questions. While there were individual variations in degrees of difference, all variations were in the same direction as the total, and confirmed the very significant deviations on both

---

[27] In this table the symbol P means precollege; C, college; G, graduate; S, the period since completing graduate work; A, academic work; O, nonacademic influences.

the Most Important Period and the Major Influence.[28] This decisive statistical evidence leaves little room for doubt that the important periods in the formulation of concepts in which intellectual issues are primary are the college, the graduate, and the after-graduate periods. These questions deal with such problems as the nature of truth, educational concepts, the relation of science to religion, and similar cognitive issues. Conversely, the period which counts for more than the other three combined in relation primarily to religious beliefs is the precollege period. Furthermore, the questions which involve a fairly even admixture of intellectual and religious issues show quite naturally a more even spread across the four periods, which is closer to the average results for all questions.

The correlations between academic and nonacademic influence are equally striking. The academic factor gains the ascendency by a slight margin on the intellectual questions, but even this small majority is so far out of line with the average for all questions that it is very important statistically. On the religious questions, the nonacademic influence is approximately six times as frequent as the academic. Again, the borderline questions stand appropriately in the middle, though even here there is a significant deviation in the direction of nonacademic influence.

The clear conclusion from these results is that basic theological orientation comes early and nonacademically, but that the intellectual refinements or modifications of this orientation take place later and under a much stronger, though not dominant, academic influence. The question remains, of course, as to where the more conservative and the more lib-

---

[28] Most Important Period: $X^2 = 1,293$; $P = .00000000000?$

Major Influence:	Intellectual Questions	Religious Questions	Borderline Questions
CR	+16.51	—21.04	—2.79
P	.00000000?	.0000000?	.005

eral religious positions represented by different teachers are to be found in terms of period and influence. Employing as our best single indication of religious belief the teachers' views of God, we present an analysis of this question in the following table.

TABLE XVI

Most Important Period and Major Influence in the Forming of
Various Views of God
(Based on totals given in Table VIII)

	Most Important Period (% of Responses)				Major Influence (% of Responses)	
	P	C	G	S	A	O
1. Christocentric View	63	13	7	15	17	75
2. Pelagian View	44	21	9	21	17	75
3. Theistic Naturalist View	19	17	14	33	21	60
4. Deistic View	32	29	14	21	21	61
5. Other Views[29]	13	29	20	13	25	36

Applying the test of Chi-square to the Most Important Periods, we found very significant deviations.[30] The theistic naturalists, the deists, and the "philosophical" groups check the precollege period far less often than their theoretical frequency for this period, while the Pelagian group is closely in line, and the Christocentric group checks this period far more often than its theoretical frequency. Conversely, the other three periods present the opposite correlations with the respective theistic concepts.

Applying the critical ratio test, the results under Major Influence are significant in the same direction, though less striking statistically.[31] The "philosophical" group represents the principal divergence here, showing a marked deviation

---

[29] To supply sufficiently large marginal totals in the respective categories for meaningful analysis, the table here presented brackets several views under what we have been terming the "philosophical" group of teachers, or Other Views. There was broad homogeneity among the subgroups within this category, on both Period and Influence.

[30] $X^2 = 61.41$; $P = .0000?$.

[31] $CR = 2.77$; $P = .006$.

toward the academic influence as compared with the rest of the teachers.

We can generalize from these results that the more conventional views of God, perhaps less modified by intellectual refinements than the others, are attributed by their bearers to early periods, with an overlapping into college, and that they derive from nonacademic factors. The more "philosophical" positions, on the other hand, stem on the whole from later periods and academic influences. This conforms with the evidence in Table XV that there is the same general variation in period and influence as between primarily religious and primarily intellectual issues.

To test this conclusion from a somewhat different perspective, we analyzed "conservative" and "liberal" views on some central theological questions in relation to Most Important Period and Major Influence. The questions for this test were selected on three bases: first, that they are clearly in the area of religion, so as not to confuse our present question with other issues; second, that they offer a sufficient division of yes and no answers to provide significant statistical data; and third, that they involve issues on which the broad lines of conservatism and liberalism as we have seen them appearing elsewhere in the study can be roughly identified by positive and negative answers. The results are presented in Table XVII.

The evidence from this table presents a strong corroboration of the conclusions which are emerging from our data. It is even more striking when statistically analyzed by individual questions and in the aggregate of the four questions. The report of this analysis will not be included here.

The chief import of these replies is that prevailingly the teachers giving the no answers, reflecting in broad terms a "liberal" view, indicate the college or graduate period as most important, the deviation for the college period being statistically significant in every case. Conversely, the results

TABLE XVII

COMPARISON OF POSITIVE AND NEGATIVE ANSWERS TO SELECTED QUESTIONS
IN RELATION TO PERIOD AND INFLUENCE
(Based on an average of 300 answers to each question)

	Most Important Period (% of Responses)				Major Influence (% of Responses)	
	P	C	G	S	A	O
9a. The Bible						
Yes Answers	70	17	7	6	16	84
No Answers	25	45	10	20	36	64
10a. The Church						
Yes Answers	75	11	4	10	9	91
No Answers	42	32	7	19	15	85
11a. Prayer						
Yes Answers	76	12	2	10	7	93
No Answers	51	29	11	9	21	79
13c. Need of Salvation						
Yes Answers	66	13	8	13	14	86
No Answers	47	30	17	6	21	79

for the precollege period deviate in the opposite direction. The graduate period, like the college period, is below expectancy in relation to the marginal totals on every question. The period since graduation runs closest to the marginal averages in the aggregate, though it is significantly above on 9a and close to significantly below on 10a. On the four questions together, the critical ratios indicate deviations which are above the marginal total for precollege but below for all of the other periods.

Under Major Influence, the evidence is self-explanatory. Though in two cases not statistically significant, in every case the deviation is in the direction of disproportionate academic influence on the negative answers, while the teachers giving positive answers attribute their views on the whole to nonacademic factors.

This concludes our analysis of the periods and influences associated with religious growth. The results on the whole have been consistent and clear. They reveal that the teachers in the study attribute the development of their religious views predominantly to the precollege and college periods, with chief accent on the former; that they are heavily indebted to nonacademic in comparison with academic influences; that broadly speaking, the more "religious" the issue involved, the earlier the period and the less academic the influence, as against later periods and more academic influences on "intellectual" issues; and that the more conservative views of God, as well as the more "positive" views on other important religious questions, arise from early periods and nonacademic influences in contrast to later periods and academic factors for the "negative" concepts.

It is not our purpose here to draw lessons from this information with respect to the training of teachers for church-related colleges. At the least it means that, if particular religious viewpoints on the part of teachers are desired, the place to begin in the development of such viewpoints is earlier than most colleges do begin or at present are able to begin. It also means that we must examine other background factors to discover their part in the process of moulding the teachers' outlooks. We shall consider first the factor of church affiliation, with a view to possible denominational differences.

Denominational Influence

Presumably a large proportion of the teachers are members of the same denominations as those in which they grew up during their formative period, and in which their religious views were moulded. In instances where this is not the case, probably the majority have transferred to their present denomination at least partly because of the greater congeniality of its outlook. In either event, therefore, the views of the teachers may be regarded as in some degree a reflection of the outlooks of their denominational groups.

With this in view, we have analyzed the replies to twenty-five questions to determine possible denominational trends. Most of the resultant information, while interesting, is not statistically significant. It is not surprising, for example, to find a heavy accent on church attendance among the Southern Baptists, the Lutherans, and the smaller evangelical groups, and a very infrequent church attendance on the part of the teachers of no church affiliation. Or again, there is a noticeable overproportion of Evangelical Lutherans, Free Methodists, and Nazarenes among those who decided to become college teachers because they regarded this as a strategic Christian vocation. These and other figures provide a confirmation of certain colorations which the study has led us to associate with certain groups, but they are not of great importance for the major purposes of our survey.

On certain questions, however, we find divergences which are worthy of note. While some of these are not statistically significant within themselves, they show cumulative trends which we must not overlook, especially since they conform at several points with data elsewhere in the study. The Congregational Christians, Methodists, Negro groups, Unitarians, and teachers of no affiliation are more "liberal" than the norm on numerous questions throughout our inquiry. On certain issues the Friends, Presbyterians U.S.A., and Episcopalians show the same trend, but on the whole these groups and the Northern Baptists and Disciples appear to represent a middle position. On the other side, the Southern Baptists, Southern Presbyterians, United Presbyterians, the Evangelical United Brethren, the members of the Reformed Church and the Evangelical and Reformed Church, and the members of the smaller evangelical denominations present a "conservative" deviation. Of the large denominations, the Methodists show the strongest trend toward theological liberalism, while the Lutherans and Southern Baptists show the greatest conservatism.

To test this observation by another set of comparable facts, we refer again to the broad correspondence we noted between denominational affiliation and views of God, where the lines of conservatism and liberalism fall *mutatis mutandis* at the same points as those we have just noted. Moreover, on Most Important Period and Major Influence the Congregational Christians, Methodists, Negro groups, Unitarians, and teachers of no affiliation register either relatively low in the precollege period or high under academic influence, conforming to the pattern of period and influence we have previously noted for the more liberal religious views. Conversely, the Southern Baptists, all Lutheran groups, and the preponderance of the smaller evangelical groups register disproportionately high either in the precollege period or in the nonacademic influence, or both. Though a test of these differences shows that they are slightly short of statistical significance, they again suggest a trend.[32]

Grouping the teachers in the three categories of the most liberal denominationally, the most conservative, and the middle group, in terms of their views of God, we find a significant difference in the major influence which they report. The most liberal veer strongly to the academic influence,[33] the most conservative approach statistical significance in the predominance of nonacademic influence,[34] and the middle group stand midway between academic and nonacademic influence.

This adds to the mounting evidence that conservative orientation in the teachers under study usually is traceable to the precollege, though sometimes the college, period, and to nonacademic influence. The liberal orientation is more often attributable to the college or graduate period and to academic influence.

As further indication of denominational differences, we discover that the Congregational Christians, the Episcopalians, the Unitarians, and those of no affiliation favor disproportionately the organization of student religious life on

---

[32] $X^2 = 11.49$; $P = .07$.
[33] $CR = +2.42$; $P = .02$.
[34] $CR = -1.87$.

an interfaith basis. The Northern Baptists, Disciples, Methodists, and Negro groups also include many teachers preferring this liberal pattern of religious work among students. The rest of the groups believe predominantly that such an organization should be Christian in purpose and program, but open in membership.

Let us note a final fact concerning denominational affiliation, namely that a cross-check of thirty-four questions on the basis of the affiliation of the colleges rather than of the individual teachers, reveals no significant differences between the two categories. It is thus consistent that the teachers in the colleges related to the smaller evangelical denominations have a disproportionate number of the theological degrees, and are very high in their checking of "strategic Christian vocation" as a motivation for becoming college teachers. The teachers in Lutheran colleges affirm strongly the necessity of church membership, disavow the goodness of man, assist students in the development of their spiritual life. Congregational Christian institutions produce strong response on the importance of the graduate period, the desirability of student and faculty participation in determining policy on religion, and the injustice of racial discrimination in selection of students.

Relatively, the teachers in Friends' schools are negative on the necessity of church membership, on the responsibility of the teacher to assist in the development of the spiritual lives of students, and on the desirability of a special Christian graduate institution, while they are positive on the interfaith emphasis and certain other "liberal" views. The teachers in Episcopal schools are negative on the necessity of church membership, on the consideration of the religious orientation of textbooks, on aiding students in the development of their spiritual life, on the propriety of a special Christian graduate institution.

Illustrations of cross-references could be multiplied. We

include here only enough to show by random sampling that the views represented by teachers of particular church affiliations correspond broadly to the views of the teachers as a whole in the colleges of the same denominations. This is not unexpected in light of the fact, as we have seen, that 56 per cent of the teachers are serving in colleges of their own denominations.

The chief disclosure of this section of our data is that the beliefs and practices of teachers differ significantly in accordance with denominational background and affiliation. It is not our task to assess which of these attitudes and activities are good and which are bad, but the college administrator looking for particular characteristics in prospective teachers will do well to consider church connection as one part of his data for predicting religious outlook and performance.

Influence of Undergraduate College Attended

In the first chapter we saw that 58 per cent of the responding teachers did their principal undergraduate work in church-related institutions, 27 per cent in tax-supported institutions, and 15 per cent in independent institutions other than those which are church-related. How, if at all, do the differences in types of undergraduate institutions which the teachers attended affect their religious beliefs and practices?

To answer this question, we divided the teachers according to the three types of institution, and ran comparisons on eighteen questions. To what extent, for example, did the three groups differ in the amount of their undergraduate academic work in religion?

The proportion of graduates of church-related colleges who took undergraduate courses in religion is significantly higher than the proportion for the other two types of institution. Fifty-one per cent of those from public institutions and 38 per cent of those from independent institutions had no work in religion at all, while only 6 per cent of the graduates of church-related institutions had no such work. Grouping the teachers in the three categories of no hours taken, one to six hours taken, and seven hours to full course taken, and applying the test of Chi-square to these replies for teachers from each type of institution, we secured one of the highest overall divergences in the study.[35] We also found significant variations of each group from the average for all the groups, though the graduates of independent institutions were closest to the norm.

These data are important if the administrators recruiting teachers for church-related colleges desire to select persons who have had—or perhaps who have not had—undergraduate courses in religion. We have a reliable basis of predictability as to where the teachers with and those without such courses are likely to be found in terms of type of undergraduate institution attended.

There are consistent differences among the three groups in other respects. Thus 59 per cent of the church-related college group reported that they decided to become college teachers partly because they considered it a strategic Christian vocation, while only 37 per cent of the group from independent colleges and 36 per cent from public colleges checked this reason. This difference suggests that the conscious Christian motivation in selecting this life work is stronger among the undergraduates in the church-related institutions than in other types of institution, but we draw no inference as to the value of this fact for their later effectiveness.

On views of God and in the aggregate response on other religious questions we find no significant differences among the teachers from different types of undergraduate colleges. But there is a deviation regarding the period of greatest importance in determining their religious beliefs.

Taking as an example the response on the concept of God,

---

[35] $X^2 = 140.48$; $P = .0000000?$.

four of the teachers from church-related colleges check the precollege period as most important to every one of this group who checks the college period. The composite figures for the teachers of the other two categories, on the other hand, show a ratio of only three for precollege to two for college. This may indicate that the students attending church-related colleges and later becoming teachers have come more largely from backgrounds in which their theological views have been fairly well set before entering college. It may also indicate that the church-related college makes less impact religiously than do other colleges. While both of these hypotheses may carry an element of truth, we do not have evidence to substantiate one or the other in our present study.

But apart from the background factor in relation to those students who become college teachers, which is our present concern, we have here a problem in relation to all students: to what extent does the church-related college exert sufficient religious impact on its students to affect profoundly their religious views? This is a subject for another study.

If there is expectation that the enlistment and preliminary preparation of college teachers should be as effective, if not more so, in the church-related college as in other colleges, two facts challenge this assumption. One is that the proportion of our respondents who decided while they were in college to become college teachers is 44 per cent for those attending public institutions, 51 per cent for those in independent schools, and only 43 per cent for church-related colleges. While these variations are not statistically significant, the fact that they give no ground for believing that the church-related institution excels in this regard is a matter of significance by default.

As a second example, the church-related college appears not to excel, and may even fall short, in its encouragement of and preparation for the graduate training of the prospective college teacher. In answer to the question, "Do you feel that you received adequate counsel as an undergraduate regarding your plans for graduate training?" the teachers from public institutions who supply definite answers divide 31 per cent yes against 69 per cent no; those from independent institutions are 37 per cent to 63 per cent; and those from church-related institutions are 29 per cent to 71 per cent. Again, there may be little significance in the discrepancies, but the fact that there is no evidence of superiority in the church-related institutions, especially when we are dealing with students who were likely candidates for return to the service of the church-related colleges and even of their own schools, is of significance in itself.

We conclude from this brief survey that the teachers who took their undergraduate work in church-related colleges had substantially more courses in religion, and that they articulate a stronger Christian motivation in deciding to become college teachers than do their colleagues from other types of institutions. On the other hand, there is no appreciable difference in their views of God or other religious concepts from those of their colleagues, and a smaller proportion regard the college period as the most important in the development of their theistic position. Moreover, the proportion of teachers who decided while in college to make college teaching their life work is slightly smaller for the church-related institutions than for the others, and the counsel provided the students in connection with their preparation for graduate training appears, according to their own evaluation, to have been less frequently adequate.

Geographical Location

We have reported earlier that the majority of the teachers are serving in the same geographical areas, divided according to the academic sectional Associations, as those in which they had their principal academic training. But whether or not this were true, it would be of interest to discover the prevailing differences, if any, in the viewpoints of teachers of different parts of the country. Geographical background may be regarded as a possible factor of influence in the teachers' outlook.

Taking first the view of God, we find no significant differences, suggesting that theological viewpoints are not conditioned dominantly by geographical setting. Other features in the determination of the teachers' theology appear to obscure or perhaps to negate whatever distinctive influence geographical location may exercise.

In certain social areas, on the other hand, the differences according to geographical location are sometimes pronounced. As might be expected, the convictions on racial issues vary widely. The best illustration was the question of admitting students regardless of ethnic considerations, on which the South presented a striking statistical deviation from the norm for the teachers as a whole.

It is not our object here to labor a particular social issue but to illustrate again that, although theistic views may vary only slightly from one geographical section to another, social views held by the same people may vary profoundly. So also may views which are religious but which are related only indirectly to theism. Thus on the relation of the college to the denomination, we find a deviation in the case of the North Central region, where the large number of teachers in the Lutheran, Reformed, and smaller evangelical denominations apparently affected the results. Here the teachers who desired a closer relation to the denomination outnumbered by more than two to one those who felt the relation should be less close, while the average ratio for all the teachers taking one or the other of these positions was about fifty-fifty. More significant was the fact that two-thirds of the teachers in all the regions combined preferred that the denominational relation remain about the same as it now is.

Other areas of comparison show the Middle States to devi-

ate. Forty-five per cent of their responding teachers have doctoral degrees, as against 35 per cent for North Central, 31
per cent for the South, and 29 per cent for the Northwest.
Only 29 per cent of the Middle States respondents when deciding to become teachers "regarded college teaching as a
strategic Christian vocation," as against 54 per cent in North
Central, 48 per cent in the South, and 71 per cent in the
Northwest. (There is no evidence of significance in the generally inverse ratio in these figures between doctoral degrees
and sense of Christian vocation.) Again, among the definite
yes and no answers as to whether the teachers assist their students "in the deepening of their spiritual life" the replies
from the Middle States are only one-fifth positive to four-
fifths negative, while the proportion for North Central is four
to five, for the South three to four and for the Northwest
fifty-fifty.

Analyzing the Middle States further, over half of their
teachers favor the interfaith type of student religious organization, whereas the ratio for North Central is one-quarter and
for the South and the Northwest is approximately one-third.
As to whether there should be a special graduate institution
under Christian auspices, the teachers from the Middle States
who provide definite answers are much more strongly opposed
than are the teachers from other areas.

The separate figures which we have cited concerning geographical differences are not significant in isolation, but in
the aggregate they indicate clearly three facts: first, that
theistic differences do not follow geographical lines; second,
that some secondary religious beliefs do correspond to geographical lines, with the Middle States showing a deviation
toward liberalism on all such issues tested; and third, that
certain racial views also show a closer correlation with geographical location than with basic theological convictions regarding the nature of God.

Academic Training

We noted in a previous reference an apparent inverse relationship in the case of the Middle States between the possession of a doctoral degree and the possession of a sense of Christian vocation in college teaching. Shall we assume from this that the higher the light of academic training, the lower the temperature of religious interest?

This conclusion does not follow. Taking first a sample question on the relation between the scientific and other possible means of arriving at truth, we made a comparison between the yes and no answers of the teachers with doctoral degrees, those with B.D. or other theological degrees and the remainder of the population in the study. The results showed no deviations of statistical significance.

Similarly, there were no significant variations regarding concept of God or the degree to which the teachers disclose their basic religious convictions in their teaching. There was an interesting difference, however, in the period regarded as most important in developing the theistic concept. Here 42 per cent of the teachers with theological degrees checked the graduate period, while only 14 per cent of the doctors and 8 per cent of the other teachers checked this period.

There is one variation from the pattern of homogeneity among holders of different degrees which is as much a commentary on human nature as a significant fact regarding teacher background. It concerns the importance attached to the doctorate. On a question regarding "the emphasis now placed by liberal arts colleges upon the Ph. D. degree as a prerequisite to teaching," over half of the doctors giving definite views replied that it is about right as it is, while a fourth felt that the emphasis is too great, and a fourth felt that it is not great enough. The teachers without a doctorate, on the other hand, registered one-third for the present emphasis, nearly two-thirds for a decreased emphasis and only 3 per cent for a greater emphasis.

Otherwise, among ten representative questions in the areas of belief, philosophy of teaching, extracurricular activities, and institutional policy, there were no significant variations. On the whole, therefore, the amount of academic training as reflected in degrees received does not appear to affect one way or the other the beliefs and practices of the teachers in the areas we are especially investigating in this study. This is not to suggest that graduate training does not improve the teacher's competence. It is merely an assertion, on the basis of the evidence, that the attainment of particular academic degrees does not consistently alter the viewpoints of the teachers on the issues of religion in relation to higher education.

When we turn from the amount of graduate training to the content of such training, we find that the data are more varied and call for more extensive analysis. Is there a measurable difference, for example, between the concepts and practices of those teachers who took undergraduate education courses and those who did not; or those who took graduate work in education, and those who did not?

One-quarter of the teachers definitely indicated they did not take education courses as undergraduates. We find no significant differences between this group and the rest of the 440 teachers in regard to their further academic progress: the number of years they did graduate study, the number of institutions they attended, the type of institutions they attended, the type of courses they took, the number of degrees they received, or the teachers' present faculty status.

Similarly, analysis of the replies of this group of teachers to ten sample questions on which an early experience in education courses might have affected their answers, shows no important deviations from the ratios for the teachers as a whole.

In addition to the homogeneity on these questions, there was broad consistency in the view of God. Perhaps more important, they showed no substantial deviations on the most important period and major influence in relation to the view of God. In short, there was no dominant educational or religious impact one way or another through undergraduate courses in education which the study has been able to isolate.

One hundred sixty, or slightly over a third of the 440 teachers, took graduate work in education. Unlike the teachers just referred to, this group show some significant differences from the teachers as a whole. We ran comparisons on forty-seven questions, involving many subquestions, to discover possible patterns of deviation. The resultant information merits consideration.

As introduction, be it noted that other possible factors which might have accounted for the differences on the part of this group of teachers, were carefully tested. Thus the proportion of doctoral degrees held by the teachers who took graduate courses in education does not differ substantially from that for the 440 teachers as a whole, being a third of the total number in each case. The 160 teachers in this group are also well distributed denominationally, both as to individual church affiliation and the church relationship of their colleges. Finally, the distribution according to subjects taught, faculty status, geographical location, and type of undergraduate college attended was compared with that for the total population of the study.

There is homogeneity in all these categories, except in two respects. First, the proportion of sociology teachers shows a significant deviation.[36] Thus the sociologists include a disproportionate number not only who have done substantial graduate work in religion, as we saw in Chapter 2, but who have done graduate work in education. However, an analysis of the total number of sociologists among the teachers we are now examining (51 out of 160) revealed that we can

---

[36] $CR = 2.71$; $P = .007$.

not attribute the findings which we shall presently observe to the high proportion of sociology teachers.

Second, we found that the 160 teachers who had taken graduate work in education included twenty-two of the thirty-nine who had had extensive graduate work in religion. Since this disproportion is statistically significant,[37] we ran a separate test of the twenty-two teachers, but found that their replies on the questions involved, like those of the sociologists, were in line with those of the 160 teachers as a whole and did not appreciably change the ratios of yes and no answers to any of the questions.

Thus the 160 teachers, tested for various possible factors which might have influenced their answers, show no serious disproportions in their composition, and may be considered as broadly representative of all the 440 teachers, except that they took graduate work in education. Therefore, in any measure that the views which they express differ significantly from the views of the 440 teachers as a whole, there may be a reasonable presumption that these differences are at least partly attributable to the effect of their graduate study in education. While we must treat the variations with caution, certain broad trends are clear. In most of the illustrations we shall supply the critical ratios as an index of their significance.

These 160 teachers are much more ready to disclose their religious conviction in their teaching than are the rest of the teachers.[38] Correspondingly, they are less fearful of dogmatism as a result of disclosing one's religious views in teaching,[39] and are more convinced that church membership is necessary to the Christian life.[40]

They lean slightly toward the optimistic view of man and

---

[37] CR $= 2.73$; P $= .006$.
[38] CR $= 2.72$; P $= .006$.
[39] CR $= 2.85$; P $= .004$.
[40] CR $= 2.62$; P $= .009$.

the compatibility of divine revelation with human reason, though in neither case significantly. On certain practical religious questions, however, they show important deviations. A larger proportion consider it a part of their responsibility to assist students in the development of their spiritual life,[41] and by nearly the same margin they favor the type of student religious organization which has commended itself historically as the pattern for voluntary student Christian expression in the church-related colleges, namely a free association of students united by a common Christian purpose and program but including interested non-Christian students in its membership. Consistent with this view, the 160 teachers in this group express a stronger sense of need for some type of faculty religious fellowship. In the same direction they present a very significant deviation toward the concept of the faculty as a closely knit Christian community or "collegium" engaged together in the enterprise of learning and teaching to the glory of God.[42] By nearly the same ratio,[43] they believe that the administration should require its faculty members to be Christian in character and conviction, though they join the rest of the 440 teachers in rejecting the tests of church membership or doctrinal conformity.

With respect to this evaluation of graduate training, it is not surprising to find those who had graduate study in education diverging from those who did not on a number of personal appraisals of their preparation for their life work. A larger proportion, relatively to the teachers as a whole, felt that their graduate work stressed broad scholarship at the expense of specialization, while a smaller proportion believed that it stressed specialization at the expense of broad scholarship.[44] They are more convinced than their colleagues

---

[41] CR = 2.64; P = .008.
[42] CR = 3.55; P = .0004.
[43] CR = 3.30; P = .001.
[44] CR = 2.21; P = .03.

that their graduate training increased their sense of the re-latedness of their subject matter to a Christian view of life, but the deviation here is not statistically significant.

The contrast in the appraisals of training for skill in teaching and in research is not decisive, but its trend is clear. The teachers who had graduate training in education are much better pleased than the other teachers with their preparation for teaching, but much less pleased with their preparation for research. As a corollary, the 160 teachers vote resoundingly for the inclusion of even further preparation for teaching in future graduate training, presenting one of the strongest contrasts in this set of comparisons.[45] In the same direction, they favor training in counseling much more strongly than do their colleagues.

The opinions expressed regarding in-service training show no conclusive evidence of differences, but they indicate a trend. On nine out of eleven options offered as desirable means of in-service training, the teachers with graduate work in education show a higher percentage of positive response, with especially high discrepancies for exchange of positions among teachers and participation in professional organizations in their teaching fields. On the other hand, the teachers without graduate work in education voted 4 per cent higher for increased opportunity for research as a means of in-service training.

Departing from the evaluation of graduate training *per se,* we find the 160 teachers considerably less certain than their colleagues that they had received adequate counsel as undergraduates in preparation for their graduate training. Though this ratio of difference falls short of statistical significance, it suggests that the teachers with graduate work in education are more alert to what ought to be done in helping prospective teachers in their plans for graduate study.

---

[45] $CR = 8.07$; $P = .0000000?$.

This group of teachers also reports greater help from the books of other teachers,[46] a fact to which we must not attach too great a significance. It is to be expected that those who took graduate work in education have read more books by other teachers about educational problems, and it is possible that the teachers who did not take such work have read books by nonteacher authors which have been equally helpful but which were not mentioned.

Thus we must treat all of these data carefully, but they seem clearly to reveal certain trends. On strictly religious concepts, the evidence we have cited in addition to the answers as a whole to strictly religious questions, indicates a slight leaning toward a "positive" religious orientation, though not sufficiently to justify important conclusions.

This evidence is more meaningful when coupled with the clear disclosure of greater practical religious concern. To a significant extent, the 160 teachers are more ready than their colleagues to disclose their religious conviction in teaching; they are more interested in faculty religious fellowship; they are more oriented toward the concept of the faculty as a Christian "collegium"; they are more convinced that the teachers in church-related institutions should be Christian in character and conviction, though free in doctrine.

With respect to training, these teachers are significantly more concerned for adequate preparation for teaching, while less concerned for preparation for research. They are more sensitive to the need for an integration of a religious view of life with their subject matter fields, and they are more committed to the in-service training of teachers. They are also more aware of the inadequacy of their own preparation as undergraduates for graduate training looking toward teaching.

As a final check to determine whether these differences are

---

[46] $CR = 2.15$; $P = .03$.

properly attributable to the graduate work in education, we tested the answers on Most Important Period and Major Influence on some of the questions where this information was asked for in the questionnaire. We found a slight though consistent trend toward the graduate period and the academic influence, as compared with the predominance of the precollege and college periods and the nonacademic influence on the part of the teachers as a whole. It may be presumed that this trend would have been even stronger in an evaluation of graduate training and other issues relating specifically to education, on which information concerning period and influence affecting their opinions was not secured.

In sum, therefore, the results of this extensive analysis of the effect of graduate work in education should be gratifying to those who are concerned for the integration of religion in higher education, and equally to those whose religious interest may be meager but who are concerned for good teaching. The evidence does not disclose as great a superiority resulting from graduate education as one might desire, but it clearly indicates that the effect of such training is in the direction of greater alertness to the issues with which both religion and education presumably are concerned.

Against this background, we examined certain other phases of academic training to discover any significant correlations with the teachers' concepts and practices. With respect to the 277 teachers who took undergraduate courses in religion, we must report, as in the case of undergraduate courses in education, that we could find no consistent correlations. Such impact as there may have been from undergraduate work in these areas appears to have been outweighed by other factors on which we have found clear correlations, such as precollege experience, denominational background, and training at the graduate level.

This brings us to specialized graduate training in religion. Our treatment again can be brief, as we presented a profile in Chapter 2 of the thirty-nine teachers who had a substantial amount of such work, and as we find the additional twenty-four teachers who did a smaller amount of such work represent broadly the same component factors.

Comparing the thirty-nine teachers who took extensive work with the twenty-four who took very limited work, we find one notable difference. The former group vary consistently and significantly from the 440 teachers as a whole in many of their views, whereas the latter group show no meaningful deviations. Since the two groups are otherwise homogenous, we may conclude that intensive graduate work in religion for periods of from one to six years clearly influenced the orientation of the teachers toward the issues with which this study deals. On the other hand, limited graduate courses in religion, involving in most cases not more than six academic hours, appear to have had no measurable effect in relation to our present concerns.

Of the thirty-nine teachers, thirty decided before or during their graduate period to become college teachers, and presumably directed their graduate study toward this objective. Correspondingly, thirty-five of the teachers did the bulk of their graduate training in religion before they started to teach, leaving only four who started their teaching first and took their graduate work in religion later.

Where do these thirty-nine teachers differ in their views from the 440 as a whole? Nine-tenths of them are in their present work because they "regarded college teaching as a Christian vocation," compared with one-half for the total population of the study. They show no significant deviations in their views of God, but one-third check the graduate period as decisive in the development of this view, whereas for the teachers as a whole, the graduate period is checked by only one-tenth of the respondents. Similarly, one-fourth of thirty-two teachers replying check the academic influence as most significant, while the ratio for the 440 teachers is one-fifth.

On a question involving both religious and intellectual concepts, namely, whether there is a basic unity in all truth, the response was so near unanimous for both groups that it need not be compared. But four-fifths of the teachers with substantial theological training reported the academic influence as most decisive in arriving at their view on this question, while the proportion for the teachers as a whole was only one-half. On the consideration of religious orientation in selecting textbooks, the proportion of the theologically trained group who respond positively is twice as large as for the total population. While this is to be accounted for in part by the high proportion of sociology and English teachers among the thirty-nine, the divergence is still notable.

The deviations are significant also in relation to certain practical bearings of religion in relation to students and to the life of the college. Two-thirds of the 39 teachers consider it a part of their responsibility to assist students in the deepening of their spiritual life through Bible reading, devotional practices, and in other ways, as against approximately one-third for the total group.

There is little difference in the proportion who feel that their institution should require its faculty members "to subscribe to a specific statement of Christian belief before being employed." This suggests that the theological training of these teachers has not, on the whole, increased their sense of the relative importance of creedal criteria in the determination of fitness for teaching in church-related colleges.

On the other hand, this group of teachers are far more committed to church membership as a requirement for faculty members than are the teachers as a whole. There is no significant deviation on the necessity of being Christian in character and conviction, indicating that all the teachers are about equally agreed on the primacy of this requirement. But more of the theologically trained teachers feel that some religious conviction is imperative, whether it be Christian or otherwise. This appears to indicate that the teachers with theological training, though placing greater stress on church membership, also attach greater value to other religious conviction which may not express itself in church membership or even in specific Christian commitment, than do the total group of teachers.

The thirty-nine teachers do not differ significantly from the rest on the issue of closer relation of the college to the denomination with which it is affiliated. This result, together with the evidence in the preceding paragraphs, indicates that the theological training of this group has not inculcated a narrow denominationalism. On the other hand, they differ significantly on an issue which is not denominational but has important Christian implications. Of the definite yes and no answers regarding the advisability of a special graduate institution under Christian auspices for the training of Christian college teachers, only three-fifths of the teachers with theological background are opposed, while four-fifths of the total group are opposed. Apparently the group who had training themselves under Christian auspices, though specifically in religious areas, are more inclined than the teachers as a whole to feel that a similar experience would be valuable for teachers generally.

A more direct self-evaluation of the teachers' graduate experience may be indicated by three questions. On the issue as to whether their graduate training provided a good balance of broad scholarship and specialization, nine-tenths of the thirty-nine teachers replied affirmatively, while for the teachers as a whole the affirmative replies were approximately two-thirds. Similarly, it is not surprising that the proportion of the theologically trained teachers who report that their Christian motivation as prospective college teachers increased during their graduate study was twice as high as for the total 440 teachers. Finally, over half of the thirty-nine teachers believe that graduate training for Christian teachers should place greater stress upon preparation for the personal counseling of students, whereas two-fifths of the teachers as a whole propose this emphasis.

This last disclosure is of particular interest in view of the fact that the thirty-nine teachers do not deviate from the average in their advocacy of greater stress on preparation for the religious leadership of students. This appears to indicate again that the teachers with substantial graduate work in religion, while more articulate and concerned regarding the Christian opportunity of college teaching, do not desire to distort higher education into an enterprise whose distinctive function is primarily religious rather than specifically educational.

Concluding our tour of academic training in its influence on the teachers' beliefs and practices, we introduce one more consideration which can be speedily disposed of. A search for possible correlations between the influence of particular graduate institutions, as well as between various groupings of such institutions, produced no positive results. Negatively, however, this disclosure indicates that generalizations regarding the religious effects of training at particular graduate institutions—with the exception of institutions of religion—are hazardous. Graduate training on the whole appears to have a consistency and inner integrity which in its overall religious impact transcends particular differences between institutions. Or if this in itself is a dangerous generalization, we can assert that the evidence in this study does not reveal what those differences may be. To discover in what degree and in what directions such variations may exist is a task for another study which would focus internally upon graduate institutions as such.

We do find from our data, however, that the influence of different fields of study, if not of particular schools, is very pronounced. In relation to the concerns of this study, we have noted significant differences between those who have had graduate work in education, and those who have not. We have analyzed also the important differences between those who have had substantial graduate work in religion and those who have not. We shall next compare the teachers according to the subjects they teach and according to their faculty status.

Subjects Taught

Observations in preceding chapters and in the foregoing section of this chapter have prepared us for certain differences in the views of the teachers according to their subject-matter fields. Since this is a conditioning factor it needs to be recognized, but since it is not a factor of background and training so much as a matter of total current orientation and interest, we shall treat it briefly. It is so interwoven in the teacher's total outlook that the relation of cause and effect as between subject and religious views is difficult to distinguish.

A fact we have previously noted is that twenty-four of the thirty-nine teachers who took one year or more of intensive graduate training in religion are teaching sociology, and that these twenty-four comprise one-third of the seventy-six sociologists in the study. Accordingly, we find the sociologists registering heavily on general questions of broad Christian motivation and interest. A check of these questions reveals that the teachers with graduate training in religion account for some, but not all, of the discrepancy. The sociologists as a whole indicate a more religious orientation, particularly in areas where human values are involved, than do the 440 teachers as a whole.

Thus three-quarters of the sociology teachers report that one of the reasons they entered college teaching was that they regarded it as a strategic Christian vocation, while one-half of the economics and physics teachers and two-fifths of the English teachers check this motivation. Similarly, 80 per cent of the sociology teachers who give definite replies state that they disclose their religious conviction in their teaching, while 72 per cent of the economics teachers, 70 per cent of the English teachers, and 59 per cent of the physicists answer this question positively.

Discrepancies in the same direction and to approximately the same extent are registered by the sociology teachers in favor of considering the religious orientation of textbooks, assisting students in the development of their spiritual life, placing greater stress on training for student counseling, and other measures designed to relate religion more closely to education.

Yet the existence of the concern in these areas does not indicate the direction which it may follow. The sociology teachers, including those with graduate training in religion, are as sharply divided as the other teachers on such issues as the necessity of church membership, the nature of man, the compatibility of divine revelation and human reason, the distinguishing marks of a Christian, the danger of dogmatism in introducing religious views into teaching, the sense of personal need for faculty religious fellowship, the merits of chapel attendance, the racial criterion in the selection of students, the desirability of a closer relationship of the college to the denomination, the evaluation of the balance of broad scholarship and specialization in their own graduate training, the effect of their training upon their Christian motivation, the merits of establishing a special graduate training institution under Christian auspices, and numerous other questions on which comparisons were run.

The clear conclusion from this evidence is that interest in persons, specialization in sociology, and even intensive training in religion do not guarantee any particular viewpoint as the end result of the process. Numerous indeterminable personal and environmental factors exercise the ultimate influence. Even on the view of God, there were no statistically reliable differences on the basis of subjects taught or, among the sociologists, on a breakdown of those with and those without religious training. We did find that the sociologists, both with and without theological study, gave greater credit to the graduate period and the academic influence as factors in determining their theistic concepts than was the case with the rest of the teachers.

As a random sample of the division among the sociologists concerning the direction of their religious and educational philosophy, we may take the question on the "one sure road of access to truth." Here it was the English teachers, not the sociologists, who departed from the norm for the teachers as a whole. In line with comments of English teachers which we quoted in Chapter 3 concerning the relation of religion to their subjects and to scientific method and other closely related topics, the English teachers veer significantly away from the proffered description of access to truth, while the physics teachers incline toward its acceptance. The sociologists and economists are in the direction of the physicists, but by a small margin.

In keeping with our analysis in Chapter 3, the rejection by many English teachers of the "scientific" definition of the means of access to truth is not to be attributed primarily to their religious orientation, but rather to their high appreciation of the place of inspiration, insight, intuition, and kindred qualities in the human spirit. Reference to this fact is not intended to discount the validity of these teachers' objections, but rather to caution against an assumption that the rejection of the proffered statement by some of the teachers was necessarily on religious grounds.

As further evidence that the English teachers consider their subject itself, with its humane associations and values, as carrying important religious implications, we cite their significant deviation from the rest of the teachers on a revealing question. Asked whether they find that their opportunity to exert a religious influence upon students through extracurricular contacts, as compared to their opportunity through academic contacts, is greater or less great, the teachers stating a definite preference vote as follows: English teachers, 36 per cent greater, 64 per cent less great; sociologists, 55 per cent to 45 per cent; economists, 63 per cent to 37 per cent; physicists, 72 per cent to 28 per cent.

In the case of the English teachers, there is evidence from other questions that they place less stress on religion in the traditional sense than do their colleagues. As a case in point, they reject more decisively than any of the other groups the possibility of a closer tie between the college and the denomination. Of the teachers stating definite preferences on this issue, the English teachers vote 37 per cent for a closer relationship as against 63 per cent for a less close relationship, the physics teachers vote 60 per cent to 40 per cent, sociology teachers 64 per cent to 36 per cent, and the economics teachers 86 per cent to 14 per cent.

In general, the economics and physics teachers appear to be the most conservative in their religious orientation, one or the other of these groups deviating sharply on many questions. They register the highest proportions on the necessity of church membership; they are the least fearful of dogmatism as a result of the teacher's relating his Christian views to his teaching; and they are the most favorable to the idea of a special Christian graduate institution. By significant margins, they also show the highest proportions checking the precollege period as most important and nonacademic factors as most influential in determining their views of God and their conception of the basic unity in all truth. These responses are clearly associated, as we saw at the beginning of this chapter, with religious conservatism.

Moreover, the economics and physics teachers display less sense of the relatedness of their subjects to religion than do the English and sociology teachers. Granted that from some points of view the connection may be harder to establish, and that it would be a mistake to inject religion artificially where it does not belong, nevertheless the replies on many questions indicate that the economics and physics teachers give less thought to the matter than the other teachers do. The discrepancy which we noted in Chapter 2 between the concern of the teachers in various fields for the religious orientation of textbooks may be largely accounted for by the great difference in the fields and by the manifest and understandable paucity of religious references in physics. The problem of textbooks in economics is more amenable to treatment, and is being attacked by representative leaders in the fields of religion and higher education at the present time.

But our principal point stands. There is evidence of a greater gap between the private religious convictions of the physics and economics teachers and their sense of the relatedness of those convictions to their subjects as teachers than we find with the English and sociology teachers. As one illustration, we may note the variations in the replies of the teachers of the four subjects as to whether they derive help toward their religious growth from "pondering their own subject matter in its religious bearings." The deviations of the four groups from the marginal totals for all the teachers tell their own story, the English and sociology teachers showing pronounced positive deviations and the economics and physics teachers presenting significant negative deviations.[47]

We need not adduce further evidence to show that the teachers in the four fields vary substantially in the various respects we have indicated. Nor is it our task here to say which trends are desirable and which are not, nor what should be done about them. Very little can be done in short-range terms, even

[47]	English Teachers	Sociology Teachers	Economics Teachers	Physics Teachers
CR	+2.76	+1.91	—2.03	—2.14
P	.006	—	.04	.03

if there were agreement as to what is desirable. The chief values in exposing these differences is to provide factual confirmation of some of the problems of which the alert leaders of Christian higher education are fully aware.

Faculty Status

In a similar category to that of subject differences is that of differences in rank. Again, it is not an issue of specific background or training but rather of present faculty status in its bearing, if any, on the orientation of the individual teacher to the questions we are discussing.

The most striking disclosure in this area is the greater sense of assurance regarding the relation of religion to higher education on the part of the faculty members of superior rank in comparison with those of lower rank. Thus on the question as to whether the teachers disclose their basic religious conviction in their teaching, the differences are significant. Subdividing the professors in order to identify those who are also deans and department heads, we find the latter two groups apparently blending assurance with administrative caution and hewing close to the average for all the teachers. The other professors, who are far more numerous, as well as associate professors, deviate in the direction of disclosing their views, while the assistant professors and instructors shy off in the opposite direction. The most cautious by far are the instructors. In like manner, the instructors are the most fearful of dogmatism if one relates his Christian views to his teaching.

Concerning administrative policy, the instructors again are conservative. On the question as to how the institution's religious policy and practice should be determined, as many instructors vote for administrative action alone as for a combination action by the administration and the faculty. This 50-50 split is in contrast to an overall vote of more than four to one in favor of administration and faculty together as against the administration alone. No other category of teachers departs significantly from this average for the teachers as a whole.

Reverting to a human interest note which we mentioned early in this chapter, there is a striking correspondence between enthusiasm for the doctorate and faculty rank. Among the teachers who state definitely that they feel the present emphasis on the Ph. D. is either too great or not great enough, the breakdown of those favoring greater emphasis is as follows: deans and department heads, 47 per cent; other professors, 22 per cent; associate professors, 12 per cent; assistant professors, 6 per cent; instructors, 6 per cent.

The information of principal importance in regard to faculty status is the increase of assurance concerning the place of religion in higher education as the teachers advance in rank. We find no correlation between this progression and specific factors of background and training. It is rather a trait associated understandably with present faculty position. It leads us, however, to a final overall examination of the teachers' opinions regarding their own background and training for their work.

Training in Retrospect

Heretofore in this chapter we have sought to identify external factors such as denominational influence, type of college attended, geographical location, academic training, subject-matter field, and faculty status in their bearing upon particular religious and educational concepts and practices of the teachers. We turn now to an examination of the teachers' own views regarding their training and the training generally of teachers for church-related colleges, without seeking primarily to isolate differences of views among different groups of teachers.

We have noted some of the factors which caused the teachers to select the particular graduate schools they attended. The factors the teachers say they would stress if they were making the selection now show significant changes. The scholastic standing of the institution in the teacher's particular field, which was a factor for 64 per cent, would be stressed now by 74 per cent; the element of the particular school of thought prevailing in the field at the institution under consideration increases from 19 per cent to 28 per cent; attention to training for teaching increases from 11 per cent to 23 per cent; for training for research, from 10 per cent to 15 per cent; the Christian orientation of the institution, from 6 per cent to 15 per cent. On the other hand, the general prestige of the institution, geographical factors, and expense or fellowship factors are now considered much less important.

Seventy per cent of the teachers felt that their graduate training presented a good balance of broad scholarship and specialization, but 41 per cent felt that it erred, if at all, in the direction of stressing specialization, while only 8 per cent felt the opposite. This is consistent with facts which we shall note presently concerning changes the teachers would now recommend in graduate training in the light of their experience.

The teachers' testimony should be reassuring to any persons sharing the apprehension of some that graduate training is destructive of religious faith. It is entirely understandable that the graduate period, in contrast with the environment of the church-related colleges which most of the teachers had attended, should offer less evidence of Christian community among the students and of Christian purpose on the part of the professors. It is also to be expected that contact with the church—and certainly with student Christian groups —should decrease during this time of intensive academic work at the graduate level. On the other hand, the observance of devotional practices neither increased nor decreased in the aggregate, and the significant average proportion of 38 per cent of the teachers reported increase in the important areas of comprehension of the purpose and opportunity of the Christian colleges, Christian motivation as a prospective college teacher, intellectual understanding of the Christian faith, and the sense of the relatedness of their subject matter to a Christian view of life. This is impressive information for the detractors of graduate training on the grounds of its menace to faith. Religious growth during graduate study may not have been as great as one might wish, but on the teachers' own testimony it is clear that the net religious impact was more positive than negative.

We have discussed previously the teachers' appraisals of the value of their training respectively for teaching and for research. We secure a simple but indicative overall perspective by noting that the number who rate their preparation for teaching as excellent is only half as great as those who rate their training for research as excellent. This ties in with their recommendation later of increased emphasis upon preparation for teaching.

It is difficult to assess the fact that only 28 per cent of the teachers felt that they received adequate counsel as undergraduates regarding plans for graduate training, whereas 56 per cent feel that prospective college teachers receive better counsel as undergraduates today. This probably means in part that such counsel has substantially improved. It may also indicate that the contrast seems greater in the light of the teachers' memories of their difficulties than it actually is. It may suggest, too, that the teachers are attempting to do good counseling, and that they interpret the situation as a whole in the light of their own efforts. In any case, it is encouraging that the teachers consider the counseling more adequate now than when they were undergraduates, as this judgment must be grounded to some degree in fact.

Beyond their evaluation of their own experience, the teachers offer important views on graduate training in general. The fact that half the teachers believe too great an emphasis is placed by liberal arts colleges upon the Ph. D. as a prerequisite to teaching, against only a tenth who believe that the emphasis is not great enough, is probably consistent with their fear of overspecialization and their relatively light advocacy of more intensive research. Whereas only 15 per cent believe that graduate training for Christian teachers in their respective fields should require more specialization in the subject, and 22 per cent propose more training in research, 70 per cent advocate a broader perspective over closely related fields, 74 per cent desire a greater integration of the subject matter in a total view of human knowledge, and 35 per cent believe there should be more training for skill in teaching. Only 12 per cent feel that this special training needs to include courses in practice teaching.

On issues of religion and human values, it is striking, as we have observed earlier, that 43 per cent advocate more training in counseling, but only 12 per cent advocate training in religious leadership. Yet 42 per cent feel that there should be greater emphasis upon the relating of their subjects to a religious interpretation of life. This set of contrasts indicates that the teachers do not consider specific religious leadership to be their professional responsibility, but they do so regard counseling. It also shows that at the intellectual level of the relation of a philosophy of religion to their teaching, in contradistinction to religious leadership more narrowly conceived, they have deep concern and a sense of responsibility for improvement.

It is a further significant fact that exactly the same proportion of the teachers, namely 42 per cent in both cases, advocate the relating of their fields more closely to social issues and to religion. The desire for clarification on social problems from a Christian point of view is a corollary of the confusion and often discouragement which, as we noted in Chapter 3, a number of the teachers confessed in other sections of the data.

That the concern of the teachers for religious orientation at the graduate level is chiefly set in the intellectual context is further indicated in the advocacy by only 5 per cent of the teachers of a student program of a religious nature as an important addition to the present graduate training program.

Consistent again is the decisive rejection, by a vote of more than three to one, of the idea of a special Christian graduate institution or institutions for the training of Christian college teachers. The reasons offered for this judgment, as well as the reasons of the minority, are worthy of study. They are presented in Appendix IV in a digested form intended to facilitate a quick overview of the arguments.

Moving from graduate training to in-service training, the teachers indicate a clear desire for more in-service training of some sort. They especially recommend supervised or directed teaching at the beginning of one's career, exchange of positions with other teachers, a more gradual introduction to full-time teaching responsibilities, increased opportunity for research, more frequent refresher courses, more participation in professional organizations in the teaching field, and specialized training and experience in personal counseling.

This brings us to the general views regarding training as volunteered by the teachers beyond the answering of specific questions. Some of these, drawn from the replies of 186 teachers, are summarized in the following table. Further condensation of these views is scarcely possible or necessary in the present treatment. They furnish corroboration and amplification, rather than modification, of the positions we have been interpreting.

In these and other comments are found indirect references to faculty qualifications in areas other than training, with a strong emphasis upon Christian character and example but a warning against creedal narrowness and indoctrination. There is a heavy accent, in one form of expression or another, upon the need for what some refer to as "great teaching." The

TABLE XVIII

Factors Listed by Teachers as Chiefly Responsible for Their
Inadequacy in Religious Areas
(Based on a total of 295 factors cited)

		% of Answers
1.	Lack of specialized training in religion and/or its relation to my field	14
2.	Lack of the aptitude, skills, social adaptability, or self-confidence necessary for dealing with students on such problems	11
3.	Lack of the necessary time and energy to deal effectively with these problems	10
4.	Lack of sufficient religious conviction and discipline	7
5.	Lack of training in counseling and human relations	7
6.	Inability to cope with rationalism, intellectual secularism, and the scientific mind	4
7.	Lack of confidence in students' religious and moral integrity	3
8.	Reluctance to intrude in the personal and religious life of students	3
9.	Insufficient personal religious background	2
10.	Lack of training in leading classroom discussion	2
11.	Limited personal contact with students	2
12.	Lack of experience in dealing with such problems	2
13.	Dealing with these matters not my proper function	1
14.	Incompatibility between my subject and religion	1

quality of the teaching represented by the respondents in this study can not be ascertained from our data. Their faculty colleagues and successive generations of students must be the witnesses to their power or lack of it as inspirers of mind and spirit.

In some respects this group of teachers is handicapped. They and their colleges are especially cramped financially. There are many poignant expressions of the gap between what they would like to do academically and what the limitation of facilities and the overburden of work allow them to do in fact. Yet there is remarkably little bitterness or despair. The mood they reflect is rather one of lingering regret.

Most of the teachers appear to be aware of their own inadequacies, which is a sign of health. They are aware also of the inadequacies of their colleagues and superior officers, which is a sign of honesty. They are eager that the training of their successors should capitalize upon the mistakes of the past.

In particular, they are desirous that men and women of promise should be enlisted for college teaching, and they are ready with suggestions as to how this can best be done. They show little enthusiasm for devices which look mechanical or organizational, such as a closer co-operation with the Future Teachers of America, the creation of a national agency to promote and co-ordinate recruitment, or even a more powerful challenge by the churches and other religious organizations. But they place strong reliance upon greater stimulation by teachers in undergraduate institutions and encouragement of the concept of college teaching as a Christian vocation. Many more of the teachers checked this last point than had checked the same motivation as a factor in their own decision to become college teachers, suggesting that they are more aware now than they were then of the power of Christian motivation as a potential influence in determining life choices.

On the practical side, the teachers believe that the recruitment of teachers for Christian higher education could be strengthened by a larger provision of fellowships for graduate training, by the promise of greater assistance in securing positions after the necessary training is completed, and especially by the improvement of salary and security provisions. Four-fifths of the teachers mention the last-named measure as against a maximum vote of three-fifths for any other point. This is another way of underlining the financial problems of the responding teachers themselves, as brought to the fore repeatedly throughout our data.

The concern of the teachers for those who are to come after them is matched by their sense of indebtedness to those who have gone before. This is expressed in their citing of the other teachers through whose articles or books their own philosophy of teaching has been enriched. Appendix V lists books of this type which were mentioned more than once. Two-thirds of the teachers indicate that they have received such help from this source, while only 7 per cent report that they have not. Two-fifths of the teachers specify books and authors, aggregating 375 listings of 211 separate titles or writers. The result is an enticing catalogue from which an interesting personal reading program could be developed by any teacher. As we noted in the case of general books of cultural or religious interest read by the teachers in the past year, the present listing is concentrated heavily on current or at least broadly contemporary writings. This applies, for example, to six of the seven authors who are listed by more than five teachers, the exception being William James. The decisive lead accorded Jacques Barzun's *Teacher in America* may be accounted for in part by the recency of its publication, while Bliss Perry's *And Gladly Teach,* which runs a strong second, was only fourteen years old at the time the teachers replied in 1949.

With our return to a discussion of the teachers' reading we are brought full circle from our original faculty profile, via their religious beliefs and contributive background factors, to a review of their opinions regarding training and finally to a look at the individual teachers in light of some of the intellectual influences which have helped to mould their professional philosophy.

In this chapter we have found that the period in which religious views were formulated, and the academic or other influences under which they developed, are important factors in moulding the teacher's religious outlook. We have seen that denominational background may be of well-nigh determinative importance. We have identified differences of effect upon the teacher's development by different types of undergraduate college attended, and different geographical backgrounds. We have discovered that undergraduate academic training in religion and in education has left no distinguish-able marks of difference upon the teachers' religious concepts and practices, but that substantial graduate training in these two fields strongly affects their outlooks on the issues dealt with in this study. We have isolated variations from the norm in accordance with subjects taught and faculty status.

Finally, we have briefly analyzed, against the background of the earlier material, the teachers' own views regarding aca-demic training, in-service training, recruitment of college teachers, important contributions to their thought by other teachers, and interrelated areas of opinion. We are now ready to attempt a summary of our findings and to draw whatever conclusions the results of this study may justify.

5.

FACULTY TOMORROW: ROAD SIGNS AHEAD

LET US remind ourselves again how hazardous it is to draw generalizations from evidence as diverse and as subject to distortion as that which we have been treating. Religious opinion is an inexact subject matter for analysis by statistical methods, and the problem of written communication increases its elusiveness. In the foregoing interpretation we have sought to strike a balance between two objectives. On the one side, we have tried to picture the broad lines of belief and practice which appear to predominate. On the other side, we have been mindful of minorities on every issue, varying in strength from one per cent or less of the total to proportions so high as to constitute nullifying divergences. We have attempted to give due regard, without pedantry, to such minorities, and yet not to magnify their significance in a way that would obscure the main currents of opinion.

Though mindful of the hazards, we must attempt now to focus the principal findings of our study, and to formulate the major issues which these findings present. We shall restrict ourselves to issues which can be functionally stated, embracing problems of action. We are emboldened to make this summary and to formulate the resultant questions by virtue of the confidence and interest expressed by the teachers. Those who have supplied the data have demonstrated their concern by their participation, and most of them have requested a report. In any measure that we may misinterpret their convictions, we ask their forgiveness.

Faculty Profile

There is further ground for our effort in the fact that the teachers, though widely diverse, are for that reason representative. They are drawn from seventy-three colleges of twenty-nine denominations in every section of the country where church-related colleges flourish. They come from institutions both old and young, small and large, co-educational and restricted to men or to women, institutions which are academically at the peak and others whose accreditation at present is regional rather than national.

Ninety-five per cent of the teachers are related to thirty-four denominations, and 4 per cent are not church members. Their aggregate church affiliation corresponds broadly to the aggregate number of teachers from the colleges of the same denominations. Fifty-six per cent of them are teaching in schools of their own affiliation. They constitute a cross-section of the faculties of their respective institutions in the amount of their academic training, the number of advanced degrees they hold, and their spread in faculty status.

Perhaps of greatest importance, these teachers are representative in terms of the subjects they teach. By design, none of them are in the field of religion. They are drawn from the three fields which are most common to the church-related colleges—the humanities, the natural sciences, and the social sciences. The first is represented by English, the second by physics, and the third by sociology and economics.

The basis of determining what teachers should be given an opportunity to participate in the study was one which reduced to a minimum the element of selection on the basis of particular interest or viewpoint. Sixty per cent of the teachers who received the instrument completed and returned it.

The one thing which all the teachers have in common is that they are serving in undergraduate, four-year, liberal arts colleges related to Protestant churches. But it is not the colleges, nor the churches, which are under study. The concern of this survey is the religious beliefs and practices of the teachers.

What caused these persons to become college teachers in the first place, and when did they decide to do so? The great majority list, in order of frequency, the appeal of teaching as such, the special attraction of working with college students, primary interest in the subject matter, and a desire to add to the body of human knowledge. One-half of the teachers gave as a further reason their conception of college teaching as a strategic Christian vocation. The predominant personal influence in their decision to become college teachers was that of their professors, with parents and other members of their families running a poor second. The influence of ministers and other religious leaders or organizations was reported as a factor in the decisions of less than one-tenth of the teachers.

The majority decided to enter college teaching while they were in college or graduate school, and most of them hoped at that time to serve in a church-related college. Nearly 90 per cent, whether or not they had a definite type of institution in mind at that time, are teaching in the type of institution they now prefer. In this and other ways they show general satisfaction with their present schools, though they freely disagree with some of their policies and practices.

The most common complaint is directed against the handicaps imposed by the financial limitations of the college and hence of its staff and facilities. There is little evidence that this difficulty is so great in the teachers' minds as to outweigh the attractions and the sense of opportunity in the church-related institutions, but many of the faculty members are under too heavy a sense of pressure and stricture to enable them to do their best work. They are concerned about the financial problem not so much as it affects them and their families personally but as it militates against their effectiveness as teachers.

A particular problem resulting from the financial stringency of the colleges is the under-staffed faculties and administrations. The teachers report not only a heavy teaching load but a taxing burden of concomitant duties. They find it difficult to keep abreast in their fields, to say nothing of doing original or creative work. Beyond the tasks assigned to them by the administration, or arising naturally from their teaching, 90 per cent of the teachers give substantial time voluntarily to counseling, both academic and nonacademic. Nearly an equal number contribute liberally of their energies to extracurricular activities with students.

On Sundays, and frequently on other days, the majority of the teachers give time to their churches. Of the 95 per cent who are church members, one-half of those giving definite information carry special responsibilities in the life of their congregations.

Due in part to these claims upon their time, the teachers on the whole reflect a lack of attention to their professional self-improvement. They are doing relatively little research, and are writing few articles or books. A large majority are members of one or more professional societies, but there are uneven reports concerning the helpfulness of these associations. Some are openly critical of such groups and their activities. Eight out of ten of the teachers report some kind of inservice training since they started to teach in college, but they indicate that these efforts often have been ineffective. There is a widespread conviction that the colleges should address themselves more aggressively to the problem of in-service training.

Equally serious is the difficulty the teachers encounter in finding the time for personal enrichment through reading, meditation, and the refreshment of their spirits. Only one-half of them report books on cultural or religious subjects outside their fields which they have read during the last year. The average number of books or authors cited by this half is less than three per person. Most of the reading reported, while not inferior, is not the most profound or searching. It corresponds in general to the best-seller selections of the public. The same observation applies to choices of magazines.

Thus apart from the problem of time, there is a problem of taste and discipline. The more basic and certainly the classical writings, whether in art, literature, science, philosophy, history, social analysis, religion, or other fundamental areas of thought and knowledge, appear to make way in the teachers' reading for secondary sources, digests, interpretations, popularizations and above all for books that are current as against those that have been tested by time. It may be assumed that more basic works comprised a larger share of the teachers' reading in the period of their academic training, but most of these undoubtedly were within their fields of special study.

Academically, the 440 teachers graduated from 248 different colleges, of which 58 per cent are church-related, 27 per cent are public and 15 per cent are independent but not church-related. All except two of the teachers have had graduate work and nearly two-thirds have studied in two or more graduate institutions. The 440 teachers attended 196 separate institutions after completing college, with a total of 910 attendances, or an average of 2.1 per teacher. The principal concentration, however, is among less than thirty institutions, with the University of Chicago far in the lead. All but 8 per cent of the teachers have degrees above the bachelor's, 54 per cent have the master's but no higher degree, 3 per cent have the B. D. or other theological degrees, and 35 per cent have a doctor's degree. More than two-thirds of the B. D. and master's degrees were received before starting to teach, while less than one-third of the doctor's degrees were received before starting to teach.

Faculty Religion

There can be little question from the evidence that the

teachers on the whole are at least conventionally religious. For the most part they give what one may term the "right answers" from the church's standpoint on specifically religious or theological issues. Only 3 of the total group, or less than 1 per cent, are avowed atheists. One-half of those who give definite replies accept the most conservative of seven proffered definitions of God, taken largely from the Apostles' Creed, while 87 per cent of the total number subscribe to one or another of four definitions which are generally within the Christian tradition. The remainder hold views which may or may not be considered Christian by the theologians. The teachers themselves in most cases regard themselves as Christians, only 2 per cent stating that they do not so regard themselves.

On other questions with a clear theological or religious import, the teachers show the same trend toward conformity. Only 14 per cent definitely reject the proposition that the Bible is religiously authoritative, 13 per cent do not regard prayer as necessary to the Christian life, and 14 per cent do not believe that all men stand in need of divine salvation through Christ. They are more sharply divided on the necessity of church membership as a part of the Christian life, 36 per cent replying negatively, and 54 per cent positively, the remainder being uncertain. The reluctance to identify the Christian life primarily with its institutional or doctrinal expressions is even more pronounced in the agreement by 73 per cent of the teachers that "what makes a man a Christian is neither his intellectual acceptance of certain ideas nor his conformity to a certain rule, but his possession of a certain spirit and his participation in a certain life." The overall answers, however, may be regarded as religiously conservative.

We must not confuse conservatism with fundamentalism. On the issue of science and religion, for example, only 8 per cent of the teachers believe that there are irreconcilable con-

flicts between the Christian religion as they understand it and
the findings of science or history in their subject matter fields.
Some of this small minority are to be found among the theologically "emancipated," who are not so fearful of scientific
domination as they are of doctrinal intransigence. The great
majority of the teachers affirm that there are differences of
method between science and the apprehension of religious
truth, but that the conclusions resulting from the differing
methodologies must ultimately be compatible. Moreover, only
5 per cent of the teachers believe that their religious faith
places limitations upon their objective search for and communication of truth in their subject matter fields. In short,
the conflict between science and religion as it raged a generation ago appears to have spent its force in these church-
related colleges. Similarly, religion as a whole and education as a whole have achieved a positive harmony, at least
on the surface.

On the other hand, the baffling conflict between certain pre-
cepts of religion and certain conscious or unconscious assumptions of education continues to create confusion. The
teachers themselves appear in the main to be unaware of the
inconsistencies, but their unawareness only adds to the problem. As a case in point, we find that 70 per cent of the teachers consider divine revelation, as they understand it, to be
compatible with human reason as a valid means of access to
truth, while only 10 per cent clearly believe that it is incom-
patible. Yet of the same 440 teachers, 65 per cent agree, and
only 24 per cent disagree, with the following statement:
"There is but one sure road of access to truth—the road of
patient, cooperative inquiry, co-operating by means of observation, experiment, record, and controlled reflection."

This inconsistency suggests that within the area of religion
the teachers are prepared to accept avenues to truth which
they explicitly or implicitly, and consciously or unconscious-
ly, disavow when they enter the area of education. The readi-

ness with which the majority accept the above statement as comprehending the means of access to truth, is evidence of the penetration of the "scientific" method into the teachers' thought processes when they are thinking educationally. To point this out is not to question the validity nor the imperative importance of the scientific approach to truth, but simply to cite the subtle assumption that it is the "*one* sure road of access to truth."

Another important and closely related case in which the religious views and other views of many of the teachers come into conflict is in their concept of man. Though an overwhelming majority believe that man stands in need of divine salvation, and in other ways affirm human dependence upon God, a majority of the teachers believe that "man is fundamentally good and his inherent goodness is indicated in his increasing capacity, by using his intelligence, to solve the problems that confront him." While there are partial explanations and perhaps justifications of this inconsistency, it reflects a widespread co-existence of theological "orthodoxy" and sociological or in some cases humanistic "liberalism" in areas which the teachers apparently do not recognize as having theological implications.

The illustrations just given are borne out by other data. There is extensive evidence in the teachers' replies that the dichotomy between their thought processes when thinking religiously and when thinking educationally has counterparts in practical activity. There is a widespread failure to integrate religious belief with either the philosophy or the practice of teaching. Religion and education appear often to reside in two watertight compartments, with no dependable line of interaction between them.

The bifurcation is equally striking in relation to day-by-day teaching choices. Shall the teacher disclose his religious conviction when it bears upon his subject, or shall he conceal it? Sixty-three per cent of the teachers reported that they disclose their conviction, leaving more than one-third who either definitely do not do so or who do not indicate that they do. The disposition to conceal their religious beliefs is especially pronounced with the teachers whose views are at variance with those of the majority. On a series of typical questions, only 29 per cent of the minority group indicated that they disclose their conviction, while on the same questions 75 per cent of the majority group disclose their conviction.

Only 2 per cent of the teachers feel that their institutions restrict them in the expression of their views on controversial religious issues, yet only 60 per cent "seek to present in broad terms a consistent intellectual interpretation of their religious faith through their teaching." The evidence indicates that four chief factors account for the hesitation of the teachers to disclose their religious convictions. First, the teachers on the whole are not skillful in formulating their religious convictions, and are reluctant to do so. Second, if they do consider it their duty to articulate their views, many of them do not consider that the classroom is the place to do it; they regard religion as an incursion into their subject matter and their teaching functions. Third, many of them find it more natural to communicate their religious conviction in extracurricular contacts and other informal relationships than through their teaching. Finally, they consider their chief responsibility in the area of religion to be that of presenting an upstanding personal example of religious belief and moral rectitude. Again, therefore, the conception of an integration of their personal faith with the intellectual discipline and the academic duties of their life work as teachers is not vividly in the consciousness of most of the teachers in this study.

There is a similar lack of carry-over from religious conviction to social conviction. While 90 per cent of the teachers believe that the pursuit of truth in their fields carries an obligation to relate that truth to the social order, and 42 per cent believe that graduate training should place greater emphasis upon the relation of their subject matter to social issues, only 57 per cent of the teachers participate in the leadership of activities which they consider to be of social or political import in their communities. A negligible number, in listing the problems which they consider important in the relation of religion to higher education, make references to the impact of their teaching or of the life of their institution upon social issues.

Equally striking is the lack of correlation between specific theological beliefs and social convictions. There is no discernible correspondence, for example, between concepts of God and attitudes on social issues, nor between denominational affiliation (or nonaffiliation) and social viewpoint. If anything, the teachers holding the "orthodox" theistic positions show less concern for social injustices than do those of the more "liberal" positions.

We find also that theistic or other theological concepts do not determine the extent of the teacher's concern for religious self-expression and personal growth in community with faculty colleagues. Despite the fact that only one-fifth of the teachers are aware of groups for this purpose on their campuses, one-half feel that such a group would be helpful to them personally. Yet this half represents a broad spread of theistic positions, indicating that a sense of need in this area is not dependent upon theological viewpoints.

It is impossible to conclude from the study which of the teachers are more effective and which are less effective as teachers. But measuring them by the tests of apparent zeal for truth, conscientiousness of purpose, respect for the personality of their students, assumption of responsibility in the life of the college community, creativity in their educational ideas, concern for self-improvement in their profession, and other clues to their industry and alertness, we must report no distinguishable differences according to theistic or denominational classifications.

Not only is the carry-over from particular theological views to particular educational views and practices impossible to establish, but there is great incongruity among the theological views themselves within a given group of teachers. It is particularly notable that the basic view of God, which we may consider the point of departure for a theology, does not predetermine what the teachers will think about the Church, prayer, the Bible, revelation, salvation, the nature of man, and other closely related questions of religious significance. Personal factors of background influence appear to be far more determinative of theological orientation than do any intellectual processes directed toward the achievement of theological consistency.

On the basis of this evidence, it can not be assumed that a particular theology will lead to a particular philosophy of religion in higher education, if to any such philosophy at all. Presumably the church-related college is concerned that its teachers shall have a religious orientation consistent with the purposes of the institution. But the important place where this orientation must be expressed if it is to reach the students effectively is in the educational philosophy and practice, not the isolated and unrelated private religious convictions of the teachers. At some point in the training process, religion and education must be brought together in the teacher's intellectual frame of reference, else his personal beliefs can not effectively serve the purposes of the college through his work as a teacher.

Faculty Preparation

What, then, are the background factors which appear to be decisive in preparing the teacher for service in a church-related college? It is notable that the basic religious orientation stems chiefly from precollege experience. On seven primarily religious questions, 58 per cent of the teachers considered the precollege period as most important in the determination of their views, 19 per cent cited the college period, 9 per cent the graduate period and 14 per cent the period since completion of their graduate work. It is apparent from these figures that fundamental religious convictions in the majority of cases have not greatly changed since the years of adolescence.

On the other hand, concepts involving an elaboration of these basic beliefs in terms of educational insights and methods are traceable predominantly to later experience. Thus on ten questions dealing with the interrelation of religious and intellectual concepts, only 15 per cent of the teachers cited the precollege period as most important, while 34 per cent gave credit to the college period, 27 per cent to the graduate period, and 24 per cent to the period since completion of their graduate work.

Similarly, the major influence to which the teachers attributed their views on the two types of questions showed a correlation as between primarily academic and primarily nonacademic factors. Fifty-three per cent of the teachers cited the academic influence as determinative on the intellectual questions, whereas only 17 per cent cited the academic influence on the clearly religious questions. It is worthy of note that even on the intellectual issues the academic influence was regarded by only approximately half of the teachers as having been decisive in the determination of their views.

It is clear from these data that, while formal educational influences at the college level and above can have a large part in the shaping of religious views, basic patterns have been established at an earlier age. The later and academic influences will in most cases effect at best a modification or enrichment of views previously held, rather than a fundamental transformation of beliefs.

The evidence discloses further that the teachers attributing the greatest importance to later periods and academic influences are for the most part those whose religious views are more "liberal," or sometimes negative. This poses an important question for the church-related college. Can and should it secure as teachers persons who hold conservative religious views, without integration of these views in terms of intellectual and educational concepts? Or can and should it secure persons who have harmonized their religious and intellectual positions, perhaps at the expense of their undiluted early religious outlook? Is there any process by which the teachers can gain the benefit of intellectual refinement and enlargement of their views without sacrificing the vitality of their religious faith?

This study can not answer this question, as it has dealt with results rather than with the means of producing or averting these results. Yet several disclosures have emerged. On the negative side, there is no significant correspondence between religious beliefs and the geographical location or origin of the teachers. There also is no apparent correlation between religious views and attendance by the teachers as undergraduates at a public, independent, or church-related college.

Similarly, we find that undergraduate courses in religion and in education, if they affected at all the teachers' beliefs and practices in relation to a philosophy of religion in higher education, show no distinguishable influence upon the teachers' present outlooks in this area. Such impact as there may have been has either been negated by other influences or so caught up in them that it can not be isolated as a significant factor.

At the graduate level, the teachers' religious beliefs and practices appear to have received no consistent impact through advanced study at particular institutions or types of institutions, except those which train primarily in theology. Nor does the amount of graduate work or the number of degrees received show any correlation with present religious views.

On the other hand, one nonacademic factor and two academic factors had significant effect in helping to mould the teachers' beliefs and practices. The first is their denominational background. There is clear correlation among the majority of the teachers between the degree of their conservatism or liberalism and their denominational affiliation. While generalizations must be subject to great caution, the Congregational Christians, Methodists, Negro groups, Unitarians, and teachers of no affiliation are more "liberal" than the norm for the teachers as a whole on numerous theological, educational, and social issues raised in this study. The most striking deviation is on the theological issues.

On certain questions the Friends, Presbyterians U. S. A., and Episcopalians show the "liberal" trend, though on the whole they are found in a middle position, together with the Northern Baptists and Disciples. On the other side, the Southern Baptists, the Southern Presbyterians, the various Lutheran groups, and the members of the smaller denominations present on the whole a "conservative" deviation. There is thus a strong degree of predictability concerning the teachers' religious outlook in accordance with their denominational background.

There is also a broad correspondence between the degree of conservatism or liberalism of a denominational group as a whole and the period and influence which the teachers consider most important in the development of their views. The groups holding a "liberal" position usually consider the later periods and the academic influence to have been determinative, while the more "conservative" groups tend to check the precollege period and nonacademic influences. Thus the correspondence which we noted earlier in the case of individuals is borne out according to denominations.

Academically, the first of the two extensive tests showing significant correlations concerns the 160 teachers who had graduate work in education, compared with the 280 who did

not report such work. The group with this training indicate
a greater concern for the integration of their subjects with a
religious view of life. They are more ready to reveal their
religious conviction in their teaching, and they are less fearful of dogmatism and other dangers as a result of such disclosure. They show more concern for their students as persons, and are more ready to help them in the development of
their spiritual life. They also give greater encouragement to
student initiative in voluntary religious activities, and express
a greater sense of the importance of similar fellowship groups
for faculty members. In the same direction, they indicate a
deeper conviction concerning the place of the Church in the
Christian life. In short, they show a greater concern for the
relating of their religious beliefs to their associations with
other persons, whether in the classroom, the faculty or the
Church.

In their philosophy of religion as it relates to higher education, the teachers with special graduate training in education present a significant deviation toward the concept of the
faculty as a closely knit Christian community or "collegium"
engaged together in the enterprise of learning and teaching to
the glory of God. They also exceed the expected frequency in
their conviction that the administration should require its faculty members to be Christian in character and conviction. Yet
they do not give evidence of narrow creedal emphasis or
sectarianism.

The 160 teachers' evaluations of their own graduate training is worthy of note. They are more convinced than their colleagues that their graduate study increased the sense of the
relatedness of their subject matter to a Christian view of life.
They are better pleased with their preparation for teaching,
though less pleased with their preparation for research. They
are stronger advocates of greater preparation for counseling,
and show a very high deviation in their advocacy of better
preparation for teaching. They have sharper convictions con-

cerning the importance of in-service training, have been influenced more deeply by the writings of other teachers, and in general show a greater alertness to the issues of higher education.

The second type of academic background showing significant influence on present belief concerned the thirty-nine teachers, chiefly sociologists, who had taken substantial graduate work in religion, amounting to a minimum of one year and in most cases three or more years of specialized study. The theistic concepts of this group showed no homogeneity, indicating that their graduate training in religion did not develop a common mind on basic theological problems. It is evident that any one seeking to learn the theological orientation of a teacher must not ask whether he had theological training, but *what* theological training he had.

But this specialized training had consistent results in other respects. It sensitized the teachers to theological issues, including the bearing of these issues on a philosophy of education, and it made the teachers more articulate and less defensive on religious questions. A disproportionate number of this group regard their present work as a strategic Christian vocation, consider the religious orientation of the textbooks they use, feel it to be a part of their responsibility to assist students in the deepening of their spiritual life, and believe that there should be a special graduate institution or institutions under Christian auspices for the training of teachers to serve in church-related colleges.

The deviation regarding a special Christian graduate institution does not appear to denote either an exclusive denominationalism or an other-worldliness on the part of this group of teachers. Their attitudes on other issues, such as the religious requirements for faculty members, the closeness of the college to the denomination, and the type of voluntary student religious program they prefer, shows no significant variations from the teachers as a whole. Thus their greater advocacy of a special Christian graduate institution probably is attributable not to narrowness but to their own favorable experience in institutions of this type, and their belief that the same values could obtain in Christian institutions training other teachers for church-related colleges.

These thirty-nine teachers make an interesting evaluation of their own graduate training. A much larger proportion than for the teachers as a whole report a good balance of broad scholarship and specialization, and state that their Christian motivation as prospective college teachers increased during their graduate study. They are also more concerned about preparation for personal counseling. Yet they do not exceed the average in the proportion advocating greater stress on preparation for the religious leadership of students. This and other evidence appears to indicate that the teachers with substantial graduate work in religion, while more articulate and concerned regarding the Christian opportunity of college teaching, agree with the teachers as a whole that the distinctive role of the church-related college is the education of the whole person, including the religious areas of his life, but that this is not primarily a religious, but an educational, role. They do not regard the teacher's function to be that of specialized religious leadership.

There are certain differences of view according to subjects taught. On the whole, the sociologists show the greatest concern for the integration of their religious beliefs with their subject matter and their teaching practices. The English teachers are more inclined to feel that their subject itself, reflecting all phases of the human spirit, embraces as much religion as is proper to the classroom. We have noted one English teacher who states, "Literature has, for me, taken the place of organized religion." The physics and economics teachers tend to be the most conservative in their theological beliefs, and also to show the least awareness of the relation of their beliefs to their teaching.

Faculty status does not appear to affect religious belief. But it does make a striking difference in teaching *practice* in relation to belief. The professors and associate professors, apparently more sure of themselves than their junior faculty colleagues, disclose their religious views more readily in their teaching, and in other ways carry their beliefs more directly into their professional life, than do the instructors and assistant professors.

The data of this study reveal, in short, that basic religious orientation comes early in life and that the chief nonacademic influence in determining the nature of religious belief is denominational, undoubtedly including the influence of the home and other precollege factors. The principal academic influences making an appreciable difference in belief, particularly in its bearing on educational concepts and practices, are at the graduate level, namely through specialized study in education and in religion. It has not been possible through this survey to isolate other factors in teacher preparation which make a demonstrable difference in religious outlook. The field of teaching and the rank of the teacher exert certain influences, but these two factors can not, strictly speaking, be considered as faculty preparation. They have to do with present faculty environment.

Shaping the Future

It is not the province of this study to distribute praise for what is praiseworthy nor blame for what is blameworthy. Nor is it our task to propose a program of improvement. In any measure that the foregoing analysis provides needed facts, it will have served its function.

Without attempting an appraisal, let us formulate certain problems about the future which the facts make inescapable. We shall state the issues in the form of recapitulations and questions, directed to all who are interested in the church-related colleges. They are formulated functionally, in the sense that they pose questions not only of theory or principle, but involving decisions regarding action.

1. We are dealing with colleges which by virtue of their church connections, and from other evidences, may be considered as having Christian objectives. But many teachers do not gain from their administrations or from any other source a clear understanding of what those objectives are. Some feel that the administration makes its position clear, but they disagree with it.

> THE ISSUE: *Should the church-related colleges seek to make clear to their faculties the distinctive objectives of Christian higher education as they conceive them, or is it better education and better Christianity to leave the formulation of Christian objectives and the application of Christian principles to the discretion of the individual teachers?*

2. The great majority of the teachers regard themselves as Christians. On the whole, their beliefs on specific religious issues are in line with widely accepted and historically transmitted positions. They appear to hold these views honestly, but often they do not consistently integrate them in a total view of life nor apply them in relation to practical issues. Frequently the teacher's growth in religious concepts has not kept pace with his intellectual development in other areas. In many cases, there is a dichotomy between theological beliefs and beliefs in areas which the teacher does not consider religious.

> THE ISSUE: *Shall it be the policy of the church-related college to encourage in its faculty members a religious conformity which is approved by the community and the constituency of the college, or shall it be the policy to employ teachers whose religious views may be less conventional but perhaps more vital and more in-*

tegrated in a total philosophy of life and of personal responsibility?

3.   The lack of an integrating religious *Weltanschauung* expresses itself specifically in relation to educational philosophy and practice. Most of the faculty members conceive their Christian responsibility as teachers to reside chiefly in two areas: that of personal Christian example and that of help to students in the development of their Christian character. There is little evidence of a profound intellectual wrestling with the problems of relationship between faith and fact, "revealed" truth and "scientific" truth, religious method and educational method, religion and an integrated curriculum. Few of the teachers report in their reading any books dealing with a Christian philosophy of higher education. Only a minority consider the religious orientation of prospective textbooks. Many are opposed to the disclosing of religious views in teaching.

> THE ISSUE: *Should the church-related colleges help their teachers through guided reading and other methods to integrate their Christian belief in some consistent manner with their educational philosophy and practice as teachers, or would such an effort result in undesirable indoctrination?*

4.   Most of the teachers report an inadequate and often ineffective in-service training program after employment. There is little evidence of a concerted or widely practiced strategy of improvement in professional competence, whether for skill in teaching, skill in research, skill in counseling, skill in religious leadership, cultural self-improvement at the teacher's initiative, or other areas.

> THE ISSUE: *To what extent is the preparation of the teacher the function and responsibility of his graduate training, and to what extent is it a function of the college which places him on its faculty?*

5. Fifty per cent of the teachers "feel the need of intimate, informal discussion and fellowship with other faculty members around common religious interests." Yet groups for such a purpose exist on campuses represented by only seventeen per cent of the teachers. Fifty-four per cent of the teachers believe that the faculty "should seek to be a closely knit Christian community or 'collegium' engaged together in the enterprise of learning and teaching for the glory of God through devotion to his truth." Yet only thirty-four per cent believe that the faculties of their institutions so regard themselves.

Here are great gaps between aspiration and realization in the spiritual-intellectual comradeship of college teachers in Christian institutions. Many teachers feel isolated from their colleagues and lonely in their religious concerns. There is an opportunity to draw together for mutual strengthening and greater effectiveness large numbers of faculty members who are separated but desire to be united.

> THE ISSUE: *Should concerted efforts be made to draw religiously interested teachers into a closer spiritual and intellectual comradeship and if so, whose responsibility should it be to exert such efforts?*

6. The training of the college teacher begins when he is an undergraduate, if not before. The majority of the teachers in the present study attribute their decision to become college teachers to the influence of their own professors. The majority did their undergraduate work in church-related institutions. Yet the group of teachers from church-related colleges reported with greater frequency than those from the public and independent institutions that they had received inadequate counsel as undergraduates on their plans for graduate training.

> THE ISSUE: *Should the church-related colleges give more attention to the enlisting of promising students for college teaching, even though most of them will*

*not return to the same college, half of them will not
teach in a college of the same denomination, many of
them will not serve in church-related institutions, and
some of them will never become college teachers
at all?*

7. Fifty per cent of the teachers assert that one of the reasons they decided to enter college teaching is that they considered it to be a strategic Christian vocation. Now, sixty-three per cent believe that the enlistment of promising teachers for Christian higher education for the future could be improved by stressing the concept of college teaching as a Christian vocation.

The church-related colleges presumably have Christian objectives. Those teachers who consciously serve these objectives may be said to have a sense of lay Christian vocation in their chosen life work. The evidence in the study does not indicate that the colleges are wholly successful in communicating this concept of their mission.

THE ISSUE: *To what extent would the encouragement
of the view that college teaching is a lay Christian
vocation be likely to enlist the right and the wrong
type of candidates, and what would be the effect of
this concept upon the performance of present teachers?*

8. Undergraduate courses in religion and in education appear to have made little difference in the teachers' present philosophy and practice in regard to religion, to education or to the interrelation of religion and education. This may be a commentary on the deposit left generally by these courses. It is clearly a commentary on the deposit left specifically in relation to present concepts of teaching held by these former students in church-related institutions.

THE ISSUE: *Could or should the church-related colleges
make provision through specialized undergraduate
courses in education, religion, or other areas for the*

preliminary preparation of teachers for church-related colleges; or should this be left to the better equipped, but perhaps not similarly oriented, graduate institutions where the prospective teachers are to do further study?

9. At the graduate level, there is evidence of a permanent impact resulting from courses in education. On the whole, this impact is in a direction which the church-related college presumably would welcome. There is a greater awareness of the interrelation of religious and educational values, a greater readiness to disclose religious convictions in a manner consistent with sound educational processes, a greater alertness to the underlying issues of higher education, a greater interest in students as persons, and a greater concern for the enlistment and adequate preparation of teachers.

THE ISSUE: *What is the role, if any, of the responsible leadership of Christian higher education in influencing the character of education courses in all types of institutions at the graduate level, and in encouraging prospective teachers for the church-related colleges to take such courses?*

10. The teachers who did substantial graduate work in religion reflect the impact of this specialized training. They show many of the same characteristics as those who did graduate work in education, and also a greater religious maturity, a deeper religious concern, and a more articulate religious consciousness than the teachers as a whole. Yet they do not display a theological narrowness nor a disregard of sound educational method. On the contrary, their awareness of educational issues is more profound than that of the teachers as a whole.

THE ISSUE: *Should church-related colleges encourage their prospective teachers, in some or all subject mat-*

ter fields, to take graduate work in religion, with special reference to the relation of religion to higher education, and to their particular subjects? If so, where and how?

11.   A closely related question is that of the advisability of establishing a special graduate institution or institutions under Christian auspices for the training of teachers for church-related colleges. The vote of the teachers in the present survey on this question was overwhelmingly negative, though an impressive array of arguments was marshalled for both viewpoints.

> THE ISSUE: *Should the Protestant churches, or perhaps their boards of education, colleges, or other agencies or leaders related to higher education, establish a graduate institution or institutions under Christian auspices for the specialized training of prospective teachers for church-related colleges?*

12.   One major reason why more of the teachers do not consider the religious orientation of textbooks, according to their replies, is that in some of their subject-matter fields few if any texts with such orientation are available. Many, though not a majority, of the teachers question whether the religious "slanting" of material in their fields would be legitimate. Many of the teachers warn against the dangers of sectarianism, dogmatism, obscurantism, the substitution of piety for sound scholarship, and other similar hazards if religion is related to the teaching of their subjects.

> THE ISSUE: *Could and should textbooks in most fields be written for specialized use in the church-related colleges, designed to reflect the broad lines of the world-view of Protestant Christianity where such is germane to the subject and where it does not obstruct the free search for and communication of truth?*

13. Many of the teachers, irrespective of subjects taught, textbooks used, and personal religious orientation, fail to effect a carry-over from their theological beliefs to social issues. This applies to the area of concept, where questions were asked concerning social convictions on specific problems; to the area of personal participation in community activities of social or political import; and to the area of the teachers' judgments regarding the role of the college in relation to social issues. While some of the teachers appeared to show little concern in these areas, others were concerned but felt that their colleges or perhaps their faculty colleagues and students were not. Some of them desired further guidance on social problems.

> THE ISSUE: *What is the responsibility, if any, of the church-related college in relation to the shaping of the social order, the advocacy and practice of social justice, and particularly the sensitizing of its teachers to the issues of society as they relate to the respective subject matter fields and to the personal role of the teacher?*

14. We have noted the correspondence of certain theological beliefs to certain denominational groupings. We have also seen that specifically religious beliefs, particularly those which are "conservative," are formulated early in life—predominantly in the precollege period, to some extent in college, and to a lesser extent in the graduate period and after completion of graduate work. This poses a difficult question concerning the relation of the college to the denomination with which it is affiliated, and to the total religious development of prospective and actual students. The normal line of procedure is for the college to accept whatever students it receives, and to do with them what it can during the college years.

> THE ISSUE: *To what extent can and should the colleges*

work with the churches and other forces in the pre-college Christian education of those who will enter college and whose religious orientation is so largely determined before they reach college?

15. Ninety per cent of the teachers attempt to give assistance in some manner to the students who desire their help on religious problems and activities, either individually or in groups. They consider that these unofficial contacts represent their best opportunity, next to their teaching (and many say in preference to their teaching) to exert a religious influence upon their students. Here is one of the places where some of the shortcomings of earlier religious training, or lack of it, might be overcome.

Yet a large proportion of the teachers consider themselves ill-equipped for such leadership, and doubt the effectiveness of their help. Many of them question the value of religious programs conducted by the administration, such as chapel services. Others are critical of the students' own efforts through their voluntary religious activities. Eighty-three per cent of the teachers prefer nondenominational to denominational student programs, but many express the fear of existing denominational pressures.

THE ISSUE: *As a part of the total strategy of Christian higher education, how can the administration, teachers and students be caught up together in a sense of meaningful Christian community around common loyalties and shared experience in campus religious life?*

These are but a few of the issues which this study poses in relation to the religious beliefs and practices of teachers. The summary may appear unduly negative. The background material in the questionnaires abounds with evidence of the vitality of most of the teachers in the colleges under study. The recapitulating of some major unanswered questions is not to depreciate the teachers. On the contrary, the issues are drawn largely from the expressions of their own concern, and reflect widespread sensitivity to the problems.

To state certain issues disclosed by this study is not to resolve them. Nor does it imply a particular viewpoint regarding the right and wrong answers. The teachers themselves are the persons from whom the answers must come. Most of them clearly indicate that they are concerned and can be counted upon to wrestle with the problems. The leaders in Christian higher education have cause for gratification in this concern and in the reservoir of Christian influence which it represents. It is the task of all such leaders, including the teachers, to seek ways of tapping this reservoir and releasing a vast potential of Christian faith and life in the colleges which is not now being used in proportion to its possibilities, nor in proportion to the teachers' own desires.

The principal religious and intellectual issue disclosed by this study is the dichotomy between Christian faith and concepts on the one side and educational philosophy and practice on the other. How can the two become one? How can the teacher, looking to God as the source of truth, communicate such of the divine light as is vouchsafed to him in a way that causes his students to know whence it comes? How, in a word, can he make his life work a testimony to the divine order?

Basic here is the issue of Christian vocation. It is the problem of every Christian—how to keep firmly planted in the two co-existing worlds of religious experience—the world of men, which God so loved for both its depravity and its divinity that he has ever sought to save it; and the world of his Kingdom, where truth is undefiled. It is the issue of so investing one's life as to help make manifest the larger life of ultimate reality. It calls for a profound conception of the Christian mission in the world.

The students, the professors, the administrators, and all others who share in the enterprise of Christian higher education partake of the character of both worlds, as do all men. Let them be aware of this, to the end that they may neither withdraw from the visible world nor be confined to its boundaries. Let religion and education be brought together. Let the teacher in particular know himself as the servant of a truth that is one and eternal, springing from God. But let him seek without apology to make this one reality manifest to a world that is divided and self-destroying because it has sought the fission of truth.

Appendices

———

Bibliography

———

Index

THE COLLEGE TEACHER AND STUDENT RELIGION

Factors in the Training of Teachers in Church-Related Colleges
which Affect the Teachers' Concepts and Practices
in Interpreting Religion to Students

A Yale Study on Religion in Higher Education

with the Cooperation of

The National Protestant Council on Higher Education
The National Council on Religion in Higher Education

The Purpose of This Questionnaire

The role of the teacher is basic to effective higher education. Church-related and other Christian colleges in the United States, and the Boards of Education of leading denominations, desire to assist college teachers to exert a constructive religious influence upon their students. As a means to this end, it is important to secure information concerning the concepts and practices of the teachers themselves regarding this problem. In particular, it is necessary to discover insofar as possible the training factors which have influenced the views and activities of present teachers, so that the training of future teachers may be guided accordingly.

Some of the basic questions on which we should like to secure factual data are:

1. To what extent does Christian higher education in the United States have a clear philosophy and purpose?

2. What are the views of college teachers concerning their role in Christian higher education?

3. In what degree do college teachers regard themselves as equipped for this role?

4. What changes, if any, should be made in the training programs for teachers in Christian colleges?

The following questionnaire has been developed in consultation with college teachers and administrators, and with leaders in graduate school education. It is being sent to teachers in Christian colleges in selected fields of study other than the field of religion. You and colleagues in your department have been chosen as one of three groups in your institution to complete the questionnaire. It will be a great service to higher education if you are able to give the time that will be required for the thoughtful answering of these questions. The validity of the study will be determined in large measure by the number and thoroughness of the replies. Your answers will be anonymous and will be held in strictest confidence by the analysts of the data.

In order that we may know whether you have replied, without knowing which is your questionnaire, will you please sign and mail the enclosed post-card when you send the questionnaire? We shall then be glad to acknowledge your cooperation and later to send you a summary of the findings. When you have had opportunity to fill out the questionnaire, will you please mail it, in the return-addressed stamped envelope enclosed, not later than April 16, 1949, to:

R. H. EDWIN ESPY,
DIRECTOR OF THE STUDY,
YALE DIVINITY SCHOOL,
409 PROSPECT STREET,
NEW HAVEN 11, CONNECTICUT.

New Haven,
March 15, 1949.

PART A — BACKGROUND INFORMATION

1. Name and location of institution in which your are teaching:...

2. Number of years you have served in this institution:...

3. Previous positions you have held in higher education:

		Subjects Taught
Institution	*Dates Served*	*(Or Other Major Responsibility)*

4. Present teaching field:...

5. Your faculty status (Professor, Instructor, etc.):...

6. Number of hours you are teaching weekly:...

7. Average number of hours weekly in research or laboratory work, preparation of lectures, reading of papers, academic counselling of students, and all other duties directly related to your teaching:.......................................

8. Average number of hours weekly in counselling of students on personal, non-academic problems:
   a. As a responsibility officially assigned to you by the administration:...............hours weekly.
   b. As a voluntary help to students:...............hours weekly.

9. Average number of hours weekly in other official duties: ....
   Character of such duties, such as committee work, chaperoning, etc., (Briefly):

10. Average number of hours weekly in voluntary extra-curricular activities with students:...............   .
    Character of such activities (briefly):

11. Your Church affiliation (Baptist, Congregationalist, etc.):...

12. Your Church attendance (Approximate frequency per year):...

13. Average number of hours weekly you devote to activities in your Church:...

14. Title of position or positions, if any, which you hold in your Church:...

Academic and Other Training

15. Institutions in which you studied *before* you started to teach in college:

Institution	*Dates*	*Major Subjects*	*Degrees*

Undergraduate:

Graduate:

16. Institutions in which you have studied *since* you started to teach in college:

Institution	*Dates*	*Major Subjects*	*Degrees*

Questions

17. Semester hours you have taken in education courses: *Undergraduate*   *Graduate*
Courses in the philosophy, history, theory, psychology or method
of education: (Specify subjects.)

Courses in practice teaching:

18. Semester hours you have taken in religious subjects (specify subjects):

19. Non-academic in-service training you have had since you started to teach college: (Check thus √ at the left
of the appropriate answer.)
.... a. Combined teaching and study (as a teaching fellow or otherwise).
.... b. Supervision of your teaching.
.... c. Informal seminars, conferences, etc., related to your subject.
.... d. Seminars, conferences, etc., related to the philosophy and method of teaching.
.... e. Projects to increase your effectiveness in counselling or other personal work with students.
.... f. Projects to increase your effectiveness in religious work with students.
.... g. Other in-service training activities. (Please specify.)

20. Some of the books on cultural or religious subjects outside your field which you have read in the last year:

21. The chief magazines on cultural or religious subjects outside your field which you read regularly:

Factors Which Influenced Your Vocational Decision

22. When did you decide to become a college teacher?
.... a. Before you entered college?
.... b. When you were an undergraduate?
.... c. During your graduate training?
.... d. Other? (Specify time.)

23. What subject did you originally expect to teach?...

24. If you have changed your field, what were your reasons for changing?

25. Why did you decide to become a college teacher? (Check not more than five reasons in order of importance,
with a 1, 2, 3, etc.)
.... a. You were primarily interested in the subject matter.
.... b. You desired to work with college students.
.... c. You felt that you would enjoy teaching as such.
.... d. You wanted to add to the body of human knowledge.
.... e. You regarded college teaching as a strategic Christian vocation.
.... f. You were attracted by the prestige, security and associations of college life.
.... g. You hoped to move from college teaching to college administration.
.... h. You were offered a teaching position.
.... i. Other. (Specify reason.)

Questions

26. Were you influenced to become a college teacher primarily by: (Check not more than five factors, in order of importance, with a 1, 2, 3, etc.)

.... a. Your parents.

.... b. One of your professors.

.... c. More than one of your professors.

.... d. Your minister.

.... e. A student religious worker on your campus.

.... f. The Student Christian Association Movement (YMCA, YWCA, SCA, etc.)

.... g. A denominational student program.

.... h. Other. (Specify factor):

27. Did you especially desire before you began teaching to teach in a particular type of institution?

.... Yes. (Specify type:)

.... No.

28. Are you teaching in the type of institution you now prefer?

.... Yes. .... No.

29. In what professional or learned societies are you a member?

30. What special leadership have you assumed beyond your institution in your field of study?

.... a. Responsibilities in professional societies:...

.... b. Articles (average number per year):.......................................

.... c. Addresses (average number per year):.......................................

.... d. Books (total number you have published):.......................

.... e. Guest lectureships in other institutions:

.... 1. Total number of lectureships:.......................................

.... 2. Extent in hours:.......................................

.... f. Recognitions, awards, etc.:...

.... g. Other leadership in your field beyond your institution:.......................................

PART B — YOUR PHILOSOPHY OF TEACHING IN RELATION TO YOUR RELIGIOUS CONVICTION

The questions in Part B of this survey call for answers in three categories:

1. Each question is to be answered in the first series of columns by a Yes, No, or Uncertain.

2. Each question is to be answered in the second series of columns by indicating the period in your life to which you attribute the greatest importance in the development of the concept or practice to which the question refers: whether pre-college (P), college (C), graduate (G), or the period since you completed your graduate work (S).

3. Each question is to be answered in the third series of columns by indicating whether the major influence in the development of the concept or practice was your academic (A) work (including the influence of school or college factors outside the classroom) or other influences not directly related to your formal education (O):

All three Columns are to be answered for most questions, but where you do not feel able to answer columns II and III, leave these blank. Answers are to be indicated by a check, thus √.

Key for replies in Column I (Basic Answer):
Y—Yes
N—No
?—Uncertain

Key for replies in Column II (Most Important Period):
P—Pre-college
C—College
G—Graduate
S—Since completion of graduate work

Key for replies in Column III (Major Influence):
A—Academic, or formal school influences
O—Other than academic or school influences

I Basic Answer	II Most Important Period	III Major Influence	Questions
Y N ?	P C G S	A O	**The Pursuit of Truth in Higher Education**

1. a. Do you agree largely with the following statement: "True education is not an end in itself but a means to an end: service to one's day and generation?"
   b. Do you believe the pursuit of truth for its own sake ever is justified in college education?

2. a. Do you believe that the pursuit of truth in your subject matter field carries an obligation to relate that truth to the social order?
   b. Do you relate the truths in your field to contemporary social problems, even on controversial issues?
   c. Do you feel that your institution allows you reasonable freedom in this regard?

3. a. Do you believe that there are irreconcilable conflicts between the Christian religion as you understand it and some of the findings of science or history in your subject matter field?
   b. If yes, do you disclose to your students the points at which you feel they must choose between science, or history, and religion?

4. a. Do you believe that some of the methods of science and of the apprehension of religious truth are different, but that their conclusions must ultimately be compatible?
   b. Do you disclose in your teaching the nature of your view in this matter?

I Basic Answer	II Most Important Period	III Major Influ- ence	
Y N ?	P C G S	A O	**Questions**
– – –	– – – –	– –	
– – –	– – – –	– –	5. a. Do you agree largely with the following statement: "There is but one sure road of access to truth—the road of patient, cooperative inquiry, operating by means of observation, experiment, record and controlled reflection?"
– – –	– – – –	– –	b. If you regard this statement to be inadequate, how would you modify it?
– – –	– – – –	– –	c. Do you interpret the realm of value as well as the realm of fact, in your subject matter field?
			6. (Answer this question only for the two fields indicated below which do *not* include your own subject, omitting either a, b, or c. Place a check before the appropriate number in each of your two replies.)

Do you believe religious truth is:

a. ....1) Equally relevant; ....2) More relevant; ....3) Less relevant, to *your* subject matter than it is to the field of the *physical sciences?*

b. ....1) Equally relevant; ....2) More relevant; ....3) Less relevant, to *your* subject matter than it is to the field of the *social sciences?*

c. ....1) Equally relevant; ....) More relevant; ....3) Less relevant, to *your* subject matter than it is to the field of the *humanities?*

Religious Belief and Teaching Practice

– – –	– – – –	– –	7. a. Do you regard yourself as a Christian, interpreting the meaning of Christian in your own terms?
– – –			b. Do you consciously disclose your basic religious conviction, whatever it may be, in your teaching?
– – –			c. Do you feel that your institution allows you reasonable freedom in the expression of your views regarding controversial religious issues?
			8. Indicate your agreement with the statement below which most nearly represents your conception of God. (Indicate by checking thus √ in the first column at the extreme left of the page, opposite the appropriate statement. Do not fail to answer this question also opposite the appropriate statement in Columns II and III.)
–	– – – –	– –	a. I do not believe in God at all.
–	– – – –	– –	b. God is a projection of human ideals and desires.
–	– – – –	– –	c. God is another name for natural law.
–	– – – –	– –	d. God is the Power making for the increase of meaning and value.
–	– – – –	– –	e. God is Absolute Mind.
–	– – – –	– –	f. God is the omnipotent Creator of the universe and of natural laws, and rules the universe through these laws. It is possible that he may be accessible to man and may be subject to man's supplications.
–	– – – –	– –	g. God is a sovereign, righteous Being, Creator of the universe and of natural laws, who through his laws rules the universe. In a special sense man is his creature, and Jesus is the supreme example of how man may know and serve God aright. The protection and favor of God can be supplicated through worship and prayer.
–			h. God is the Father of our Lord Jesus Christ, and of all mankind; Maker of heaven and earth; unto whom all hearts are open, all desires known; and from whom no secrets are hid; whom to know is perfect peace.
–	– – – –	– –	i. Other more adequate view: (Please specify.)

I Basic Answer	*II* Most Important Period	*III* Major Influ- ence	
Y N ?	P C G S	A O	**Questions**
— —	— — — —	— —	9. a. Do you consider the Bible to be religiously authoritative?
— —			b. Do you communicate your views on this matter in your teaching?
— —	— — — —	— —	10. a. Do you regard church membership to be a necessary part of the Christian life?
— —			b. Do you seek to influence students who are not church members to join a church of their choice?
— —	— — — —	— —	11. a. Do you regard prayer as necessary to the Christian life?
— —			b. Do you disclose your view on this matter in your teaching?
— —	— — — —	— —	12. a. Do you derive your concept, whatever it may be, of the worthfulness of human life and the brotherhood of man from your view of God?
— —			b. Does your view of God increase your encouragement of originality, independence and personal responsibility in your students?
— —	— — — —	— —	13. a. Do you agree largely with the following statement: "Man is fundamentally good and his inherent goodness is indicated in his increasing capacity, by using his intelligence, to solve the problems that confront him?"
— —	— — — —	— —	b. If this statement is inadequate, how would you modify it?
— —	— — — —	— —	c. Do you believe that all men stand in need of divine salvation through Christ, in whatever way you understand this concept?
— —			d. Do you disclose your views on the nature of man in your teaching?

Religious Belief and Scientific Objectivity

— —	— — — —	— —	14. a. Do you believe that your religious faith places limitations upon your objective search for and communication of truth in your subject matter field?
— —			b. Do you encourage students to avoid areas of study which you feel are inimical to their Christian faith?
— —			c. Do you allow students to pursue lines of thought and expression which are at variance with your religious views?
— —	— — — —	— —	15. a. Do you consider divine revelation, as you understand it, to be compatible with human reason as a valid means of access to truth?
— —			b. Does your religious conviction and experience lead you to insights in your subject matter field which you feel you would not possess in equal measure apart from your religion?
— —			c. Do you seek to interpret to students in your teaching some of the insights or disclosures of religion which you believe have a bearing upon your subject matter?

I Basic Answer	II Most Important Period	III Major Influ- ence	Questions
Y N ?	P C G S	A O	
– – –	– – – –	– –	

– – –	– – – –	– –	**16. a.** Do you believe there is a basic unity in all truth?
– – –		– –	**b.** In your philosophy of teaching is God, as you conceive him, the central reality underlying and lending unity to all truth?
– – –	– – – –	– –	**c.** If not, state briefly your conception of the integrating factor, if any, which should lend intellectual and moral unity to the teaching of the various subjects in college:
– – –			**d.** In your teaching do you disclose your philosophy regarding the integration of truth with a unifying order in the universe?
– – –			**e.** Do you think the educational philosophy of your institution is based on a Christian concept of God as the central reality underlying all truth?
			f. If this is not the philosophy of the institution, how may its philosophy of education in relation to a religious view of the universe be described?
– – –			**g.** Does the administration make a serious effort to disclose its philosophy in this regard, whatever it may be, to the students?
– – –			**h.** Do you feel that the faculty is consulted as fully as it should be in the determination of the educational philosophy of your institution?
– – –	– – – –	– –	**17. a.** Do you believe that one must seek an intelligent understanding of his religious faith?
– – –			**b.** Do you seek to present in broad terms a consistent intellectual interpretation of your religious faith through your teaching?
– – –			**c.** If the subject matter of your teaching sometimes undermines the religious faith of your students, do you seek to help them reinterpret and reconstruct their faith on a more adequate foundation?
			d. Do you agree largely with the following statement: "What makes a man a Christian is neither his intellectual acceptance of certain ideas nor his conformity to a certain rule, but his possession of a certain spirit and his participation in a certain life?"
			e. If you regard this statement to be inadequate, how would you modify it?
			18. Do you believe that the college professor who seeks to relate his Christian views to his teaching is in danger of:
– – –			**a.** Sectarianism.
– – –			**b.** Dogmatism.
– – –			**c.** Obscurantism.
– – –			**d.** Substitution of piety for sound scholarship.
– – –			**e.** Other characteristics:
– – –			**19. a.** In selecting textbooks for your courses, do you take account of the religious orientation, if any, reflected in the treatment?
			b. What are some of the textbooks in your field whose religious orientation you regard to be valuable for your students?

PART C — YOUR PHILOSOPHY OF EXTRA-CURRICULAR COLLEGE LIFE
IN RELATION TO YOUR RELIGIOUS CONVICTION

I
Basic
Answer

Y   N   ?

Questions

Your Personal Relations with Students

___ ___ ___ 1. Do you regard it as part of your responsibility in your extra-curricular contacts with students to help them develop their Christian character?

___ ___ ___ 2. Do you seek to assist students in the deepening of their spiritual life through Bible reading, devotional practices and in other ways?

___ ___ ___ 3. a. Do you regard it as part of your responsibility to assist your students in the selection of a life vocation?

b. Do you discuss this problem with: (Check the appropriate answer.)

................1) All of your students.

................2) Most of your students.

................3) Half of your students.

................4) Less than half of your students.

................5) Very few of your students.

................6) None of your students.

___ ___ ___ c. Do you present this problem as a matter of Christian life commitment?

4. Do you feel that your religious concepts and practices make the attainment of a sense of community with students, on the whole: (Check the answers which apply.)

.... a. More difficult.

.... b. More easy.

.... c. More fruitful.

.... d. Less fruitful.

.... e. No different than if you did not hold these religious views.

.... f. Other.

Your Participation in Student Organizations

___ ___ ___ 5. a. Do you regard it as part of your responsibility, if so requested, to aid the Student Christian Association, YMCA, YWCA, denominational foundation, or other voluntary student-faculty religious group on your campus?

b. Do you engage in such activities as the following with these voluntary religious groups from time to time? (Check the items which apply.)

................1) Giving talks.

................2) Leading Bible study.

................3) Leading discussions.

................4) Chairing forums or other meetings.

................5) Counselling or training students in organizational leadership.

................6) Counselling or training students in religious leadership.

................7) Accompanying students on deputation teams.

................8) Attending committee meetings.

................9) Assisting in program planning.

...........10) Serving as official faculty adviser.

...........11) Assisting in religious emphasis week.

...........12) Interpreting the student program to the faculty and administration.

Questions

..............13) Raising money.

..............14) Attending intercollegiate conferences.

..............15) Assuming leadership in intercollegiate conferences.

..............16) Taking students to intercollegiate conferences.

..............17) Engaging in student summer projects.

..............18) Relating the student program to the churches in the community.

..............19) Relating the student program to the YMCA or YWCA in the community, if such exists.

..............20) Relating the student program to social action or social service projects in the community.

..............21) Participating in voluntary student-faculty worship services.

..............22) Leading worship services.

..............23) Helping students relate their Christian convictions to campus problems.

..............24) Using your home for student religious meetings.

..............25) Other.

6. a. Approximately how many hours per week do you devote to the activities listed in points 1-25 in question 5?..............................hours.

    b. Of this time, approximately:

       1) How many hours represent voluntary service?..........................

       2) How many hours represent responsibility to which you have been officially assigned by the administration?..........................

7. Which of the following are ways in which you are able to exert the greatest religious influence, outside the classroom, upon students? (Check not more than five items, in order of importance, with a 1, 2, 3, etc.)

      .... a. Personal counselling.

      .... b. Leading Bible study.

      .... c. Leading other groups.

      .... d. Speaking to meetings.

      .... e. Sharing and leading in worship.

      .... f. Assisting in planning of student religious activities.

      .... g. Informal, unplanned contacts.

      .... h. Preaching.

      .... i. Entertaining students in your home.

      .... j. Serving as official faculty adviser.

      .... k. Participating in service projects.

      .... l. Participating in extra-curricuar activities other than those associated primarily with religious purposes.

      .... m. Other.

8. Do you find that your opportunity to exert a religious influence upon students through extra-curricular contacts, as compared to your opportunity through academic contacts, is, on the whole:

      .... a. Greater.

      .... b. Less great.

      .... c. About the same.

      .... d. Impossible to compare.

Questions

9. a. In your institution, do you believe that the major voluntary student religious organization should be:

.... 1. Distinctly Christian in purpose, program and membership.

.... 2. Distinctly Christian in purpose and program, but inclusive of interested non-Christian members and/or participants?

.... 3. Inclusively inter-faith in purpose, program and membership.

   b. Which of the following do you believe should be given the greater emphasis by the students and the college as a whole on your campus:

.........1) Denominational student programs, separately organized primarily for students of the various denominational affiliations?

.........2) Nondenominational student programs of a Christian character, designed to include all students who desire to participate?

The Religious Life of the Faculty

10. Do you find that your own religious growth is aided most by: (Check not more than five items, in order of importance, with a 1, 2, 3, etc.)

.... a. Courses or informal group studies in religion.

.... b. Reading the Bible.

.... c. Engaging in personal devotions.

.... d. Engaging in family devotions.

.... e. Engaging in public worship including hearing sermons.

.... f. Reading books of inspiraton on religious subjects.

.... g. Attending lectures on religious subjects.

.... h. Pondering your own subject matter field in its religious bearings.

.... i. Studying the truths of various religions.

.... j. Studying the intellectual framework and formulations of the Christian faith.

.... k. Seeking to apply your religious conviction to concrete problems.

.... l. Other.

Basic Answer
Y   N   ?

___ ___ ___ 11. a. Do you feel the need of intimate, informal discussions and fellowship with other faculty members around common religious interests?

___ ___ ___   b. Does a group for such a purpose exist on your campus?

___ ___ ___   c. Do you participate in this group?

___ ___ ___   d. Would you participate in such a group if it existed?

           12. a. Do you believe that the faculty in an institution such as yours should seek to be a close-ly-knit Christian community or "collegium" engaged together in the enterprise of learning and teaching for the glory of God through devotion to his truth?

___ ___ ___   b. On the whole, does the faculty in your institution so regard itself?

___ ___ ___   c. In official sessions of the faculty or in committees on educational policy is such an idea sometimes discussed?

___ ___ ___   d. Do you feel that the element of professional rivalry or jealousy among faculty members seriously hinders the realization of such a community in your institution?

*Basic
Answer*

Y   N   ?

Questions

The Administration and Religion

13. a. Do you believe that your institution should require its faculty members: (Please indicate your position on all the possibilities stated.)

— — —   1) To subscribe to a specific statement of Christian belief before being employed?

— — —   2) To be members of an evangelical church?

— — —   3) To be Christian in character and conviction?

— — —   4) To possess religious conviction, whether Christian or otherwise?

— — —   5) To indicate in some other way their religious orientation? (Please specify.)

b. Do you inform the administration when you disagree with its position on religious questions?

 ....1) Usually.

 ....2) Sometimes.

 ....3) Never.

c. Do you seek to inform the administration of non-conformity in the religious views of faculty colleagues?

 ....1) Usually.

 ....2) Sometimes.

 ....3) Never.

14. Do you believe that your institution should require chapel attendance on the part of:

— — —   a. Students?

— — —   b. Faculty?

15. Do you believe that your institution should require any religious activities other than chapel attendance on the part of:

— — —   a. Students? (If yes, specify such activities.)

— — —   b. Faculty? (If yes, specify such activities.)

— — —   16. Do you believe that your institution, if it has made clear to prospective students its position on religious matters, should select its students partly on religious grounds?

17. a. Do you believe that your institution's religious policy and practice should be determined cooperatively by:

 ....1) The administration, the faculty and the students.

 ....2) The administration and the faculty.

 ....3) The administration alone.

b. In which manner does your institution determine its religious policy? (Circle 1), 2), or 3) above.)

— — —   c. Have you served on cooperative committees to deal with this problem?

— — —   d. Would you like to serve on such a committee if requested to do so?

— — —   18. a. Do you believe that under existing conditions your institution should select its prospective students partly on grounds of race, color or national origin?

— — —   b. Do you feel that your institution makes as great an effort as it should under existing circumstances to recruit qualified students from the lower economic and social levels of society?

N.   ?

—   —   —

—   —   —   19. a. Do you regard it as one of the functions of your institution to help shape the character of
                   the social order in the direction of greater justice; if necessary, at risk of public criticism?
—   —   —   b. Do you believe your institution regards this to be one of its functions?
—   —   —   c. Do you participate personally in the leadership of political or social affairs in your com-
                   munity?
—   —   —   d. Do you participate officially on behalf of your institution in the leadership of political or
                   social affairs in your community?
—   —   —   e. Does your institution encourage faculty members to assist in the formulation of its policy,
                   either academic or community, in relation to controversial social issues?
—   —   —   f. Do you participate in committees or other official processes which are helping to deter-
                   mine such policy?

—   —   —   20.   Do you believe that your institution should be related to the denomination or denomin-
                   ations with which it is affiliated:
                   .... a. More closely than it now is
                   .... b. Less closely than it now is
                   .... c. About the same as it now is
                   .... d. Uncertain

PART D — YOUR VIEWS REGARDING THE TRAINING OF CHRISTIAN TEACHERS
FOR HIGHER EDUCATION

Questions

Your Own Graduate Experience

1. a. What were the major factors which caused you to select the graduate school where you secured your doctor's
      degree, or, if no doctoral degree, the institution in which you took most graduate work? (Check prefer-
      ably not more than five factors, in order of importance, with a 1, 2, 3, etc.)
      ....1. The scholastic standing of the institution as a whole.
      ....2. The scholastic standing and offerings of the institution in your particular field.
      ....3. The general prestige of the institution.
      ....4. The particular school of thought which prevailed in your field.
      ....5. The influence of a particular professor in the graduate institution.
      ....6. The institution's attention to training for teaching.
      ....7. The institution's attention to training for research.
      ....8. The Christian orientation of the institution.
      ....9. The geographical accessibility of the institution.
      ....10. Geographical change from where you lived or studied.
      ....11. Moderate expense of the institution.
      ....12. A fellowship or other financial aid.
      ....13. The views of your undergraduate professors as to where you should go.
      ....14. Other (Specify factor):

   b. Which of the above factors would you regard as most important if you had the decision to make *now:*
      (List here, in the order of importance, the numbers corresponding to the items above which you now regard
      as most important.)

   1st   2nd   3rd   4th   5th

2. a. Did your graduate training provide a good balance of broad scholarship and of specialization?
      .... Yes   .... No   .... Uncertain

   b. It erred (if at all) in the direction of: (Check No. 1 or No. 2.)
      ....1) Stressing broad scholarship at the expense of specialization.
      ....2) Stressing specialization at the expense of broad scholarship.

3.   During your graduate training: (in the institution referred to above)

	Increase	Decrease	Remain About Same
a. Did your comprehension of the purpose and opportunity of the Christian colleges:			
b. Did your Christian motivation as a prospective college teacher:	....	....	....
c. Did your sense of Christian community with fellow-students (as compared with your undergraduate experience):			
d. Did your sense of the Christian purposes of your professors (as compared with your undergraduate experience):			
e. Did your contact with the Church:	....	....	....
f. Did you contact with Student Christian Groups:	....	....	....
g. Did your observance of personal devotional practices:	....	....	....
h. Did your intellectual understanding of the Christian faith:	....	....	....
i. Did your sense of the relatedness of your subject matter to a Christian view of life:	....	....	....

4.   Was your graduate training: (Check the appropriate adjective under both a and b.)

a. For achieving the skills of teaching:
  ....1) Excellent
  ....2) Good
  ....3) Fair
  ....4) Poor
  ....5) Very Poor
  ....6) Non-existent

b. For achieving the skills of research:
  ....1) Excellent
  ....2) Good
  ....3) Fair
  ....4) Poor
  ....5) Very Poor
  ....6) Non-existent

Your Present Views on Graduate Training

5.   Do you believe that the emphasis now placed by liberal arts colleges upon the Ph.D. degree as a prerequisite to teaching is, on the whole:
  .... a. Too great
  .... b. Not great enough
  .... c. About as it should be

6.   Upon which of the following do you believe graduate training for Christian teachers in your field should place greater emphasis in the future, even if this should involve an additional year for completion of the graduate work? (Add to the list as many items as you desire, indicating the order of importance, with a 1, 2, 3, etc.)
  .... a. More specialization in the subject matter field.
  .... b. Broader perspective over closely related fields.
  .... c. An integration of the subject matter in a total view of human knowledge.
  .... d. Training for skill in teaching.
  .... e. Training for research.
  .... f. Courses in practice teaching.
  .... g. Training in the personal counselling of students.
  .... h. Training in the religious leadership of students.
  .... i. Relating your field to social issues.
  .... j. Relating your field to a religious interpretation of life.
  .... k. Maintenance of a student program of a religious nature.
  .... l. Other areas:

7. a. Do you believe that a special graduate institution or institutions should be established under Christian auspices for the training of Christian college teachers in your field?
  b. Give as many reasons as you wish for your answer:
     ....Yes   ....No   ....Uncertain
  1.
  2.
  3.

Questions

Yes	No	?	

8. Do you believe that in-service training for teachers in Christian colleges should emphasize more than at present: (Place before not more than five "yes" answers, in order of importance, a 1, 2, 3, etc.)

a. A period of internship after completion of graduate work.
b. Supervised or directed teaching at the beginning of one's career.
c. Cooperative teaching on a group basis, that is, by several teachers.
d. Exchange of positions and intervisitation with other teachers.
e. A more gradual introduction to full-time teaching responsibilities.
f. Assistance through rating and student reaction.
g. Increased opportunity for research.
h. More frequent refresher courses.
i. Participation in professional organizations in the teaching field.
j. Specialized training and experience in personal counselling.
k. Specialized training and experience in religious leadership and interpretation.
l. Other.

9. a. Do you feel that you received adequate counsel as an undergraduate regarding your plans for graduate training?

b. Do you feel that prospective college teachers receive better counsel as undergraduates today regarding their graduate training than they did when you were an undergraduate?

10. Do you believe the enlistment of promising teachers for Christian higher education could be improved by: (Place before not more than five "yes" answers, in the order of importance, a 1, 2, 3, etc.)

a. Greater stimulation by faculty in undergraduate institutions.
b. Encouragement of the concept of college teaching as a Christian vocation.
c. A larger provision of fellowships for graduate training.
d. Increased cooperation of Christian colleges with the Future Teachers of America and other organizations of prospective teachers.
e. The creation of a national agency to promote and coordinate recruitment.
f. A more powerful challenge by the churches and the Student Christian Movement, in line with the principles of the Student Volunteer Movement's enlistment for missionary service.
g. The improvement of salary and security provisions.
h. The promise of greater assistance in securing positions after the necessary training.
i. Other.

Final Reflections

1. a. Has your philosophy of teaching been enriched by articles or books by other college teachers, past or present? ....Yes ....No ....Uncertain

b. What are some of the articles or books which have helped you especially?

2. a. List the religious activities or problems with which you find yourself least able to deal adequately in the course of your work: (List one each under 1, 2, etc., not to exceed a total of three.)

1)

2)

3)

Questions

b. List the factors which you regard as chiefly responsible for your inadequacy in each of the stated areas (Indicate one major factor for each area, under 1, 2, etc., with special reference to training factors, if any.)

1)

2)

3)

13. List what you consider to be the chief weaknesses of Church-related colleges as you have experienced them with special reference to educational philosophy and faculty training:

1)

2)

3)

14. a. Do you feel that secularization of outlook in your college, as compared with ten years ago,
  1) Among the students, is:
  ....a) Greater; ....b) Less great; ....c) About the same; ....d) Uncertain

  2) Within the faculty, is:
  ....a) Greater; ....b) Less great; ....c) About the same; ....d) Uncertain

  3) In the administration, is:
  ....a) Greater; ....b) Less great; ....c) About the same; ....d) Uncertain

  b. Do you believe that the present degree of secularisation in your college is, on the whole, a healthy condition for a Christian institution of higher education in view of the secularization of the society from which the students are drawn and to which they will return?
  .... Yes   .... No   .... Uncertain

  c. List the chief measures, if any, which you feel are most needed in your college to develop a sound and effective Christian higher education for your students:

  1)

  2)

  3)

15. Will you please write on a separate sheet whatever you would most like to say regarding the college teacher's relation to religion in higher education, with special reference to training. A sheet of normal weight may be enclosed with the questionnaire without requiring additional postage to mail it.

May we thank you again for your cooperation in completing this questionnaire. We repeat: in order that we may know whether you have replied, without knowing which is your questionnaire, will you please sign and mail the enclosed post-card when you send the questionnaire? We shall then be glad to acknowledge your cooperation and later to send you a summary of the findings. When you have had opportunity to fill out the questionnaire, will you please mail it, in the return-addressed stamped envelope enclosed, not later than April 16, 1949, to:

R. H. EDWIN ESPY,
YALE DIVINITY SCHOOL,
409 PROSPECT STREET,
NEW HAVEN 11, CONNECTICUT

APPENDIX II
Distribution and Interpretation of the Questionnaires

The limitations of the questionnaire approach for an opinion survey were fully faced. By means which we need not detail here, an effort was made to offset these limitations. The number and the thoroughness of the responses were such as to vindicate the planning, and no supplementary measures for amplification of the answers were found necessary. It can not be questioned that interviews or other follow-up would have been useful if they had been feasible, but the answers and comments were so clear that additional insights resulting from a further process would have been chiefly in the realm of nuances.

Three objectives were paramount in the circulation of the instrument. The first was to reach a maximum number of teachers in the four subject fields. The second was to reduce to a minimum the possibility of discrimination or favoritism in selecting the teachers. The third was to present the questionnaires in a way that would create a desire to co-operate in the project.

All of these objectives were met in so far as possible by a single process, namely by enlisting the participation of the president. A pilot study distributed to teachers at Denison University, Maryville College, Oberlin College, and West Virginia Wesleyan College had demonstrated the value of the president's support. This sample study had also been a major help in the final formulation of the questionnaire.

After selection of eighty-one colleges on a random sampling basis the desideratum of maximum coverage was achieved by discovering the number of teachers of the four subjects in each institution and requesting the president to distribute a questionnaire to each teacher. This accomplished also the second aim of objectivity, as it eliminated the possibility of individual selection. It met the third problem by providing the explicit or implicit sponsorship of the president.

The interest of the presidents was secured in various ways, including the announcement of the project as an official Yale study, sponsorship by the National Protestant Council on Higher Education and the National Council on Religion in Higher Education, letters of support from the Protestant Council as well as from the secretaries of the Boards of Education of most of the denominations involved, and extensive personal contacts. Only one administration indicated its unreadiness to co-operate, due to a vacancy in the presidency, and completed questionnaires were received from seventy-seven of the eighty-one institutions. The survey was conducted during the spring of 1949.

The replies to the questionnaire were summarized in two hundred pages of data providing numerical results, and in seventy-nine supplementary tables showing correlations, comparisons, or other information.

This material was interpreted in three hundred additional pages of text. For permission to consult the detailed statistics and exposition as presented in the dissertation, inquiries should be directed to Professor Clarence P. Shedd, Yale University Divinity School, New Haven, Connecticut.

APPENDIX III

THE 73 COLLEGES REPRESENTED IN THE FINDINGS

(Listed according to denominations)

Advent Christian
Aurora College, Illinois

Baptist, National
Bishop College, Texas

Baptist, Northern
Bucknell University, Pa.
Franklin College of Indiana, Ind.
Linfield College, Oregon
William Jewell College, Mo.

Baptist, Southern
Blue Mountain College, Miss.
Hardin-Simmons University, Texas
Judson College, Alabama
Mercer University, Georgia
Ouachita College, Arkansas

Brethren, Church of
Juniata College, Pa.

Brethren, Evangelical United
Albright College, Pa.
Otterbein College, Ohio

Church of God
Anderson College and Theological Seminary, Indiana

Congregational Christian
Beloit College, Wisconsin
Pacific University, Oregon
Tillotson College, Texas
Yankton College, South Dakota

Disciples of Christ
Butler University, Indiana
Hiram College, Ohio
Texas Christian University, Texas

Evangelical and Reformed
Catawba College, N. C.
Heidelberg College, Ohio

Friends
Guilford College, N. C.
Whittier College, Calif.

Lutheran Augustana Synod
Augustana College and Theological Seminary, Illinois
Gustavus Adolphus College, Minn.

Lutheran, Evangelical
Luther College, Iowa
St. Olaf College, Minnesota

Lutheran Synodical Conference including Missouri Synod
Valparaiso University, Ind.

Lutheran, United
Midland College, Nebraska
Susquehanna University, Pa.
Wittenberg College, Ohio

Mennonite
Bethel College, Kansas

Methodist
Allegheny College, Pa.
Baldwin-Wallace College, Ohio
Bethune-Cookman College, Fla.
Central College, Missouri
University of Denver, Colorado
Drew University, New Jersey
Emory and Henry College, Virginia
Georgia Wesleyan College, Ga.
Hendrix College, Arkansas
Iowa Wesleyan College, Iowa
Millsaps College, Miss.
Nebaska Wesleyan University, Nebraska
Paine College, Georgia
Randolph-Macon College (for men), Virginia

THE 73 COLLEGES REPRESENTED IN THE FINDINGS (continued)

Syracuse University, New York
Western Maryland College, Md.

Methodist (A.M.E.Z.)
Livingstone College, N. C.

Methodist (Colored M.E.)
Texas College, Texas

Methodist (Free)
Seattle Pacific College, Wash.

Moravian
Moravian College and Theological
  Seminary, Pa.

Nazarene
Northwestern Nazarene College,
  Idaho

Presbyterian, United
Muskingum College, Ohio

Presbyterian, U. S.
Hampden-Sidney College, Va.
Southwestern at Memphis, Tenn.

Presbyterian, U. S. A.
Carroll College, Wisconsin
Hanover College, Indiana
Idaho, The College of, Idaho
Johnson C. Smith University, N. C.
Lake Forest College, Ill.
Lindenwood College, Mo.
Missouri Valley College, Mo.
Tusculum College, Tenn.
Whitworth College, Wash.

Protestant Episcopal
Hobart and William Smith
  Colleges, New York
South, University of the, Tenn.

Reformed
Hope College, Michigan

Seventh Day Adventist
Union College, Nebraska

Universalist
St. Lawrence University, N. Y.

ANALYSIS OF THE 73 COLLEGES

	Number	Per cent*
Denominations represented in 73 colleges	29	—
Geographical location of 73 colleges (according to the academic Regional Associations):		
Middle States	11	15
North Central	33	45
Southern	22	30
Northwest	7	10
New England	—	—
Total	73	100%
Sizes of the 73 colleges:		
Below 500 students	10	13
500- 999	46	63
1,000-2,499	13	18
2,500-4,999	2	3
5,000-9,999	—	—
10,000 or more	2	3
Total	73	100%
Negro colleges replying	7	10
Division of colleges according to co-education:		
Co-educational	66	91
Men's colleges	4	5
Women's colleges	3	4
Total	73	100%
Division of colleges according to accreditation:		
Nationally accredited	32	44
Regionally accredited	41	56
Total	73	100%

* Percentages throughout the study are given without decimals, for reasons indicated in the background study.

DIVISION OF TEACHERS ACCORDING TO DENOMINATIONS
OF 73 COLLEGES

Denomination	Number of Colleges	Number of Teachers	% of 440 Teachers (to the nearest .5%)
Advent Christian	1	7	2
Baptist, National	1	3	1
Baptist, Northern	4	27	6
Baptist, Southern	5	25	6
Brethren, Church of	1	5	1
Brethren, Evangelical United	2	13	3
Church of God	1	5	1
Congregational Christian	4	20	4
Disciples	3	30	7
Evangelical and Reformed	2	13	3
Friends	2	10	2
Lutheran, Augustana	2	16	4
Lutheran, Evangelical	2	20	4
Lutheran, Synodical Conference	1	4	1
Lutheran, United	3	24	5
Mennonite	1	4	1
Methodist	16	89	20
Methodist (A.M.E.Z.)	1	6	1
Methodist (Colored)	1	4	1
Methodist (Free)	1	6	1
Moravian	1	5	1
Nazarene	1	6	1
Presbyterian, United	1	8	2
Presbyterian, U. S.	2	12	3
Presbyterian, U. S. A.	9	46	12
Protestant Episcopal	2	15	3
Reformed	1	11	3
Seventh Day Adventist	1	1	—
Universalist	1	5	1
Totals	73	440	100

APPENDIX IV

REASONS GIVEN FOR POSITIVE AND NEGATIVE ANSWERS TO THE
QUESTION CONCERNING THE ADVISABILITY OF A SPECIAL GRADUATE
SCHOOL UNDER CHRISTIAN AUSPICES TO TRAIN TEACHERS FOR
CHURCH-RELATED COLLEGES

Positive	No. of Answers*	% of Answers†
1. Present institutions are un-Christian in emphasis	21	24
2. A Christian graduate institution might place greater stress on teaching as compared with subject matter	12	14
3. It would integrate subject matter with a Christian world-view	12	14
4. It would prepare teachers for the many specific needs of Christian colleges	8	9
5. It would broaden the concern of teachers for human problems and human relations	7	8
6. It would develop a community of like-minded graduate students and, eventually, of teachers	6	7
7. It would train prospective teachers in religious counseling and other religious leadership	4	5
8. It would help overcome the religious immaturity and pseudo-sophistication of young teachers	3	3
9. It would attract students more suitable to becoming Christian teachers	3	3
10. It would develop loyalty to the denomination and to the Church as a whole	3	3
11. It would supplement the present inadequate number of graduate schools	3	3
12. It would make a Christian impact on prospective teachers at a strategic period in their development	2	2
13. It would continue the universal search for truth under Christian motivation and orientation	1	1
14. It would counteract the legal limitations which are placed upon the teaching of religion in public-supported graduate institutions	1	1
Percentage adjustment for fractions	—	3
Totals	86	100

* All answers to Question 7b were formulated by the respondents; the captions
here given did not appear in the questionnaire; they have been rephrased and
grouped by the author.

† Based on total of 86 reasons given.

REASONS GIVEN FOR POSITIVE AND NEGATIVE ANSWERS TO THE
QUESTION CONCERNING THE ADVISABILITY OF A SPECIAL GRADUATE
SCHOOL UNDER CHRISTIAN AUSPICES TO TRAIN TEACHERS FOR
CHURCH-RELATED COLLEGES (continued)

Negative	No. of Answers	% of Answers*
1. Such an institution would isolate students from other viewpoints and from the rest of the world	47	14
2. It would endanger objective scholarship and the search for truth	36	11
3. Existing graduate institutions are adequate to the need	30	9
4. Such graduate training would be too narrow, neglecting the "whole man"; it would constitute another form of specialization, not integration	29	9
5. A student's life philosophy should be well established before he reaches graduate school, calling for no further "coddling"	25	8
6. Christianity and subject matter should not be confused with one another in graduate training	23	7
7. Such a venture would be difficult to finance; the cost is not justifiable	16	5
8. Training in such an institution would lead to theological hair-splitting, strife and sectarianism	16	5
9. Existing institutions could be adapted to meet the need	13	4
10. A "Christian" graduate institution would encourage hypocrisy and intolerance	11	3
11. It would subordinate ethics and sensitive social concern to dogmatism, separate religion from life, remove prospective teachers from a true understanding of student needs	10	3
12. It would not have adequate academic standards and facilities	10	3
13. It would not attract the best teachers to its staff	9	3
14. It would be stigmatized in the academic world; its graduates would meet difficulty in securing placement	5	2
15. It would run the danger of religious institutionalism and outside non-academic control	4	1
16. It would be undemocratic in its policy of enrollment and academic restriction	4	1
17. It would effect more mental stagnation than progress, and might become reactionary	3	1
18. The churches should first compose their differences before establishing a "Christian" graduate institution	3	1

* Based on total of 333 reasons given.

REASONS GIVEN FOR POSITIVE AND NEGATIVE ANSWERS TO THE
QUESTION CONCERNING THE ADVISABILITY OF A SPECIAL GRADUATE
SCHOOL UNDER CHRISTIAN AUSPICES TO TRAIN TEACHERS FOR
CHURCH-RELATED COLLEGES (continued)

Negative (continued)	No. of Answers	% of Answers
19. Intelligent teachers will get their own religious orientation	3	1
20. Graduate training can not make a person a Christian	3	1
21. Most teachers are already sufficiently religious	2	1
22. There can be adequate religious expression through extracurricular activities in present institutions	2	1
23. There already are too many graduate schools and teacher-training institutions	2	1
24. A good graduate institution can not be created in a short time	2	1
25. A Christian graduate institution would not attract the best students	2	1
26. The development of the Christian viewpoint is the task of the Church, not of higher education	2	1
27. A Christian graduate institution would not solve the basic problem of secularism	1	—
28. The Church does not have all the answers in this area	1	—
29. The Church should work more effectively with students in existing graduate institutions	1	—
30. So-called "Christian" social programs are often unrealistic and hence harmful	1	—
31. The real need is for training teachers who can teach undergraduates	1	—
32. Religion in the Church-related colleges should be handled by experts, not by the whole faculty	1	—
33. The undergraduate teaching resulting from training in a Christian graduate school would alienate students	1	—
34. The Christian emphasis should be made in the institution where the teacher is employed, not in the graduate training of the teachers	1	—
35. A Christian graduate institution would presuppose a religious background on the part of its students	1	—
36. The products of such an institution would not be sufficiently different to justify its existence	1	—
37. There would be too few candidates for enrollment in such an institution	1	—
38. It would be in danger of parochialism, as the teachers would have to be clergymen	1	—
39. Teachers trained in this setting would tend to assume special qualities (remember West Point and Annapolis)	1	—

REASONS GIVEN FOR POSITIVE AND NEGATIVE ANSWERS TO THE
QUESTION CONCERNING THE ADVISABILITY OF A SPECIAL GRADUATE
SCHOOL UNDER CHRISTIAN AUSPICES TO TRAIN TEACHERS FOR
CHURCH-RELATED COLLEGES (continued)

	No. of Answers	% of Answers
Negative (continued)		
40. Such a plan would entail undue additional time for the completion of one's graduate work	1	—
41. The same ends could be met by a supplementary year in an existing Christian institution	1	—
42. Such an institution might fall into the hands of "educationists" and so repel serious scholars	·1	—
43. It would narrow the choice of good teachers for Church-related colleges	1	—
44. The same objectives could be better accomplished through Christian conferences and Christian community living	1	—
45. Separation of Church and State precludes special religious instruction to veterans	1	—
46. There would be danger of confusing a "Christian" institution with anti-Semitism and related bigotries	1	—
47. Why should we develop Christians when the greatest protagonists of social justice have been non-Christians?	1	—
Percentage adjustment for fractions	—	2
Totals	333	100

APPENDIX V

The Books Written by Other Teachers Which Are Reported by More Than One Teacher as Especially Helpful

No. of Teachers*

Barzun, Jacques, *Teacher in America,* and other writings, contemporary 36

Perry, Bliss, *And Gladly Teach,* 1935 24

Dewey, John, the works of, contemporary 9

Hutchins, Robert M., the writings of, contemporary 7

Chase, Mary Ellen, *A Goodly Fellowship,* 1939 6

Cole, Luella, *The Background for College Teaching,* 1940 6

James, William, *Talks to Teachers on Psychology,* 1899 6

Arnold, Matthew, the works of, 19th century 5

Bell, Bernard Iddings, the works of, contemporary 5

Cantor, Nathaniel Freeman, *Dynamics of Learning,* 1946 5

Palmer, George Herbert, *The Life of Alice Freeman Palmer,* 1908 5

The Bible 4

Harvard Report, *General Education in a Free Society,* 1945 4

Lynd, Robert Staughton, *Knowledge for What? The Place of Social Science in American Culture,* 1939 4

Maritain, Jacques, the works of, contemporary 4

Brown, Rollo Walter, *On Writing the Biography of a Modest Man,* (the life of Dean LeBaron Russell Briggs of Harvard), 1935 3

Eliot, Charles, the works of, late 19th and early 20th centuries 3

Emerson, Ralph Waldo, the works of, 19th century 3

McGrath, Earl James, *Toward General Education,* 1948 3

Meiklejohn, Alexander, *What Does America Mean?,* 1935 3

Niebuhr, Reinhold, *The Nature and Destiny of Man; a Christian Interpretation,* 1941 3

Plato, the works of, 4th century B.C. 3

Roucek, Joseph Slabey, *Sociological Foundations of Education, a Textbook in Educational Sociology,* 1942 3

Trueblood, David Elton, *Alternative to Futility,* 1948 3

Van Doren, Mark, *Liberal Education,* 1943 3

Ames, Edward Scribner, the works of, contemporary 2

Aristotle, the works of, 4th century, B.C. 2

Brumbaugh, Martin Grove, *The Making of a Teacher; a Contribution to Some Phases of the Problem of Religious Education,* 1905 2

Chase, Mary Ellen, *A Goodly Heritage,* 1932 2

Coe, George Albert, *A Social Theory of Religious Education,* 1917 2

Conant, James Bryant, *On Understanding Science,* 1947 2

Demyashkevich, M. Khail Ivanovich, *An Introduction to the Philosophy of Education,* 1935 2

DuBois, Patterson, *The Point of Contact in Teaching,* 1897, and later editions 2

* Percentages are not given, as the figures in most cases for each book or author are too small to lend significance to a percentage breakdown.

THE BOOKS WRITTEN BY OTHER TEACHERS WHICH ARE REPORTED
BY MORE THAN ONE TEACHER AS ESPECIALLY
HELPFUL (continued)

	No. of Teachers
Edman, Irwin, *Philosopher's Holiday*, 1938	2
Einstein, Albert, the works of, contemporary	2
Eliot, T. S., the works of, contemporary	2
Erskine, John, *The Memory of Certain Persons*, 1947	2
James, William, *The Varieties of Religious Experience*, 1902, and later editions	2
Jeans, Sir James, *The Mysterious Universe*, 1931	2
Jordan, David Starr, *The Call of the Twentieth Century; an Address to Young Men*, 1903	2
Lewis, C. S., the writings of, contemporary	2
Marston, Leslie Ray, *From Chaos to Character—a Study in the Stewardship of Personality*, 1944	2
Millikan, Robert A., the writings of, contemporary	2
More, Paul Elmer, *The Greek Tradition from the Death of Socrates to the Council of Chalcedon, 399 B.C. to A.D. 451*, 1921-1927, 4 vols.	2
Newman, John Henry, *The Idea of a University Defined and Illustrated*, 1873 (3rd edition), and later editions	2
Du Nuoy, Pierre Lecomte, *Human Destiny*, 1947	2
President's Commission, Report of, *Higher Education for American Democracy*, 1947	2
Richards, James Austin, *Bible Studies*—on Jesus, Matthew, etc., contemporary	2
Russell, Bertrand, the writings of, contemporary	2
Santayana, George, *The Last Puritan*, 1935	2
Tead, Ordway, *College Teaching and College Learning*, 1949	2
Van Doren, Mark, *The Noble Voice, a Study of Ten Great Poems*, 1946	2
Winship, Albert Edward, *Great American Educators*, 1900	2
Wriston, Henry Merritt, *The Liberal Arts College*, 1935	2

BIBLIOGRAPHY

The selection of the most useful books and other publications from an extensive list of possibilities is made difficult by the varying needs of different readers. The bibliography which follows, while it reflects some of the reading involved in the foregoing study of the religious views of college teachers, is not intended as documentation of the study. It is selected primarily with a view to helping the average mature student or college teacher or administrator in a non-technical approach to the problems of religion in higher education, with special emphasis on the place of the teacher. Each of the entries is listed under only one heading, though the material in most of them overlaps several headings. The publications which are most relevant to the material in this book are indicated by an asterisk (*).

A. BOOKS

1. HISTORY AND PHILOSOPHY OF HIGHER EDUCATION

Butts, R. Freeman. *The College Charts Its Course: Historical Conceptions and Current Proposals.* New York: McGraw-Hill Book Company, Inc., 1939. 464 pp.

Conant, James B. *Education in a Divided World.* Cambridge: Harvard University Press, 1949. 249 pp.

Gideonse, Harry D. *The Higher Learning in a Democracy.* New York: Farrar and Rinehart, 1937. 287 pp.

Greene, Theodore M., editor. *The Meaning of the Humanities.* Princeton: Princeton University Press, 1938. 198 pp.

————, et al. *Liberal Education Re-Examined: Its Role in a Democracy.* New York: Harper and Brothers, 1943. 134 pp.

*Harvard Report: *General Education in a Free Society.* Cambridge: Harvard University Press, 1945. 267 pp.

Hutchins, Robert M. *The Higher Learning in America.* New Haven: Yale University Press, 1936. 119 pp.

*Moberly, Sir Walter. *The Crisis in the University.* London: SCM Press, Ltd., 1949. 316 pp.

*Nash, Arnold S. *The University and the Modern World.* New York: The Macmillan Company, 1943. 312 pp.

Newman, John Henry. *The Idea of a University, Defined and Illustrated.* New York: Longmans, Green and Company, 1912. 527 pp.

*President's Commission on Higher Education. *Higher Education for American Democracy,* A Report. New York: Harper and Brothers, 1948. 5 Vols. (various pagings).

*Tewksbury, Donald George. *The Founding of American Colleges and Universities Before the Civil War.* New York: Teachers College, Columbia University, 1932. 254 pp.

Whitehead, Alfred North. *Aims of Education and Other Essays.* New York: The Macmillan Company, 1929. 247 pp.

2. RELIGIOUS ORIENTATION

Brunner, H. Emil. *Revelation and Reason: The Christian Doctrine of Faith and Knowledge.* Tr. by Olive Wyon. Philadelphia: Westminster Press, 1946. 440 pp.

*Calhoun, Robert Lowry. *God and the Common Life.* New York: Charles Scribner's Sons, 1935. 303 pp.

Ferré, Nels F. S. *Faith and Reason.* New York: Harper and Brothers, 1946. 251 pp.

Jessup, T. E., et al. *The Christian Understanding of Man* (Official Oxford Conference Book). New York: Willett, Clark, and Company, 1938. 268 pp.

Long, Edward Leroy, Jr. *Science and Christian Faith,* A Haddam House Book. New York: Association Press, 1950. 125 pp.

*Miller, Alexander. *Christian Faith and My Job,* A Haddam House Book. New York: Association Press, 1946. 60 pp.

*Miller, Carl Wallace. *A Scientist's Approach to Religion.* New York: The Macmillan Company, 1947. 127 pp.

Niebuhr, H. Richard. *The Meaning of Revelation.* New York: The Macmillan Company, 1941. 196 pp.

Professional Life as Christian Vocation, A Report on Laymen's Institutes and Groups, published by the Ecumenical Institute, Geneva, Switzerland, 1948. 82 pp.

Thomas, George Finger. *Religion in an Age of Secularism,* the Inaugural Lecture of George F. Thomas, Professor of Religious Thought on the Herrington Spear Paine Foundation. Princeton, New Jersey, 1940. 30 pp.

*Visser 't Hooft, W. A. *None Other Gods.* New York: Harper and Brothers, 1937. 185 pp.

3. RELIGION AND HIGHER EDUCATION

American Council on Education, Committee on Religion and Education. *College Reading and Religion:* A Survey of College Reading Materials, sponsored by the Edward W. Hazen Foundation and the American Council on Education. New Haven: Yale University Press, 1948. 345 pp.

*Brown, William Adams. *The Case for Theology in the University.* Chicago: University of Chicago Press, 1938. 123 pp.

*Coleman, A. John. *The Task of the Christian in the University.* New York: Association Press, 1947. 113 pp.

*Cuninggim, Merrimon. *The College Seeks Religion.* New Haven: Yale University Press, 1947. 319 pp.

Dewey, John. *A Common Faith.* New Haven: Yale University Press, 1936. 87 pp.

Gross, John O. *Education for Life.* New York: Abingdon-Cokesbury Press, 1948. 219 pp.

Hartshorne, Hugh, editor. *From School to College: A Study of the Transition Experience,* conducted by Lincoln B. Hale, et al. New Haven: Yale University Press, 1939. 446 pp.

Hites, Laird Thomas. *The Effective Christian College.* New York: The Macmillan Company, 1929. 259 pp.

Limbert, Paul M. *Denominational Policies in the Support and Supervision of Higher Education.* New York: Teachers College, Columbia University, 1929. 242 pp.

Patton, Leslie Karr. *The Purposes of Church-Related Colleges: A Critical Study—A Proposed Program.* New York: Teachers College, Columbia University, 1940. 287 pp.

Redden, John D., and Francis A. Ryan. *A Catholic Philosophy of Education.* Milwaukee: The Bruce Publishing Company, 1942. 605 pp.

*Shedd, Clarence Prouty. *The Church Follows Its Students.* New Haven: Yale University Press, 1938. 327 pp.

Sperry, Willard Learoyd, editor. *Religion and Education.* Cambridge: Harvard University Press, 1945. 114 pp. Especially chap. iv, Victor L. Butterfield, "Religion in the Liberal College."

*Van Dusen, Henry P. *God in Education.* New York: Charles Scribner's Sons, 1951.

4. THE TEACHER

Barzun, Jacques. *Teacher in America.* Boston: Little, Brown and Company, 1947. 321 pp.

Bowman, Isaiah. *The Graduate School in American Democracy.* Washington: United States Office of Education, 1939. 70 pp.

Browne, Kenneth Alton. *The Selection of Faculty Members for Church-Related Colleges.* Philadelphia: National Protestant Council on Higher Education, 1942. 112 pp.

Cole, Luella. *The Background for College Teaching.* New York: Farrar and Rinehart, Inc., 1940. 616 pp.

Hollis, Ernest Victor. *Toward Improving Ph.D. Programs.* American Council on Education, Commission on Teacher Education. Washington, D. C., 1945. 204 pp.

*Limbert, Paul M., editor. *College Teaching and Religious Values.* New York: Association Press, 1951.

*Lowry, Howard. *The Mind's Adventure.* Philadelphia: Westminster Press, 1950. 154 pp.

Tead, Ordway. *College Teaching and College Learning, A Plea for Improvement.* New Haven: Yale University Press, 1949. 56 pp.

B. BULLETINS, PAMPHLETS, AND REPORTS

1. RELIGION IN HIGHER EDUCATION—GENERAL

Educating for Christian Citizenship: Report of Montreat Workshop. Charlotte, North Carolina: Queens College *Bulletin,* XXVI, No. 4, April, 1948.

Ends and Means in the Humanities, Proceedings of a Conference Sponsored by the Social Science Foundation. Denver, Colorado: University of Denver, 1943.

**Hazen Pamphlets,* published by the Edward W. Hazen Foundation, New Haven, Connecticut (dates in certain cases not indicated). Especially: Bixler, Julius Seelye. *The Resources of Religion and the Aims of Higher Education,* 1942; Braisted, Paul J. *Religion in Higher Education;* Calhoun, Robert L. *The Place of Religion in Higher Education;* Livingstone, Sir Richard. *Some Thoughts on University Education,* 1948; Niebuhr, Reinhold. *The Contribution of Religion to Cultural Unity,* 1945; Shedd, Clarence P. *Proposals for Religion in Postwar Higher Education,* 1946; Shuster, George N. *Education and Religion,* 1945; Tead, Ordway. *The Relation of Religion to Education: A Layman's View,* 1944.

*Holbrook, Clyde A. *What Is a Christian College?,* published as edition of *Social Action,* XV, No. 7, September 15, 1949.

Latourette, Kenneth Scott. *Can We Keep Our Christian Schools and Colleges Christian?,* a pamphlet printed for private circulation by the Baptist Board of Education, New York.

Pike, James A. *The Place of Religion in a University.* Reprint of Opening Sermon as Chaplain of Columbia University, New York, 1949.

Wedel, Theodore O. *The Church and the University,* published by the Committee on College Work, Province of Washington, D. C., of the Protestant Episcopal Church.

*Wygal, Winnifred. Synopsis and Study Outline for the Book *The Crisis in the University,* by Sir Walter Moberly. New York: National Intercollegiate Christian Council, 1950.

2. RELIGION IN HIGHER EDUCATION—TEACHING

**Hazen Pamphlets,* published by the Edward W. Hazen Foundation, New Haven, Connecticut. Especially: Malin, Patrick Murphy. *Teaching Economics With a Sense of the Infinite and the Urgent,* 1942; Nason,

John W. *The Program of Faculty Consultations on Religion in Higher Education*, 1946; Outler, Albert C. *Colleges, Faculties and Religion*; an appraisal of the Programs of Faculty Consultations on Religion in Higher Education, 1945-48, published 1949; Tead, Ordway. *Spiritual Problems of the Teacher*, 1945.

Mosier, Karl H. *College Teacher Supply and Demand:* Report for the North Central Association of Colleges and Secondary Schools, 1948.

New School for Social Research. *Bulletin* of the Graduate Faculty of Political and Social Science, V, No. 8, 1948-49.

*Religious Perspectives of College Teaching. A Series of Essays published by the Edward W. Hazen Foundation, New Haven, Connecticut, in 1950. Religious Perspectives: (1) *In English Literature*, Hoxie N. Fairchild; (2) *In History*, E. Harris Harbison; (3) *In Economics*, Kenneth E. Boulding; (4) *In Philosophy*, Theodore M. Greene; (5) *In the Classics*, Alfred B. Bellinger. Manuscripts are now in preparation for additional Essays to be published in 1951 on: Education, Political Science, Cultural Anthropology, Experimental Psychology, Physics, Biology, Music and Fine Arts, and Law. The Series is to be available in book form in the fall of 1951.

Report of Consultation on the Preparation of College Teachers. Prepared for private circulation by the Edward W. Hazen Foundation, New Haven, 1947.

Selection and Placement of College Teachers, The. Report of a Conference of Officers of Liberal Arts Colleges and Universities under the Auspices of the Cooperative Bureau for Teachers, New York, 1948.

Smith, Elliott H., editor. *Education for Professional Responsibility.* New York: Carnegie Press, 1948.

Southern University Conference, *Report of the Committee on the Improvement of Instruction*, 1947.

University of Chicago Committee on the Preparation of Teachers. *The Preparation of College Teachers, A Statement of Policy and Plans*, 1948.

C. SELECTED NONDENOMINATIONAL JOURNALS WHICH CARRY FREQUENT OR OCCASIONAL ARTICLES ON RELIGION IN HIGHER EDUCATION

American Journal of Sociology, The
American Scholar, The
Bulletin of the Association of American Colleges
Christian Century, The
*Christian Education
Christianity and Crisis
Der Christliche Student, Journal of the German Student Christian Movement, Stuttgart

Ecumenical Review, The, Quarterly of the World Council of Churches, Geneva
Educational Record, The
Intercollegian, The
Journal of the American Association of Collegiate Registrars
Journal of Bible and Religion
Le Semeur, Journal of the French Student Christian Movement, Paris
Motive
Religious Education
Religion in Life
School and Society
Student Movement, The, Journal of the Student Christian Movement of Great Britain and Ireland, London
*Student World, The, Quarterly of the World's Student Christian Federation, Geneva

INDEX